MW01130753

Lodge Cast Iron Dutch Oven Cookbook for Beginners 1000

The Ultimate Guide of Lodge Cast Iron Dutch Oven Recipe Cookbook for Healthy Effortless Savory Lodge Cast Iron Dutch Oven Dishes

By Jenny Kenze

Table of Contents

Introduction

The Lodge Cast Iron Dutch Oven is a multi-functional cookware that works wonders with slow-cooking recipes and all your favorite foods. The Lodge Cast Iron Dutch Oven holds a heap of chili, chicken and rice, or fruit cobbler.

This model features a flat-bottom and sits on the stovetop burner or coven, with a domed lid that sends moisture back into the pot. Loop handles aid in carrying with oven mitts. Cast-iron retains heat well so you can sear meat at higher temperatures and will keep your delicious meals warm for a long time.

Whether used in a kitchen or camp, theses virtually indestructible cookware should last for generations. Made of cast iron, this Lodge Cast Iron Dutch Oven evenly distributes heat from the bottom through the sidewalls.

Sporting a stylish black color, the cast iron Lodge Cast Iron Dutch Oven looks good in most kitchens and it doubles up as an excellent source of nutritional iron. This Lodge Cast Iron Dutch Oven is ready-to-use right out of the box. While the cookware comes pre-seasoned to prevent food from sticking, it works best when sprayed or lightly coated with vegetable oil before use.

The Lodge seasoning procedure is a multiple-step process in which the seasoning oil is applied via an electrostatic spray system that coats the cookware, then it's baked in commercial ovens at very high temperatures. This allows the oil to penetrate deeply into the pores of the iron. This seasoning process achieves a seasoned finish that would take many months of home use to achieve. Sometimes during this process, the seasoning oil can collect and create a bubble or slight drip at the bottom of the pan as it's hanging through the production process. And that in turn can turn brown as it's processed through the seasoning ovens. This brown spot is not rust but in fact, carbonized seasoning and will darken with use.

The factory seasoning process makes Lodge cast iron products ready to use right out of the box, and the product over time "Just keeps getting better". After cooking, clean with a stiff nylon brush and hot water. Using soap is not recommended, and harsh detergents should never be used. Towel dry immediately and apply a light coating of oil to utensil while it is still warm.

Cast Iron, like your grandmother used, still ranks as one of the best cooking utensils ever made. It gives you a nearly non-stick surface, without the possible harmful fumes generated by preheating chemically treated nonstick cookware. The American-based company, Lodge, has been fine-tuning its construction of rugged, cast-iron cookware for more than a century.

Making The Most Of Your Lodge Cast Iron Dutch Oven

In the early days of the American colonies, Lodge Cast Iron Dutch Ovens were a kitchen workhorse. Their durability and versatility made them a valuable tool both inside farmhouse kitchens and outdoors at explorers' camps. In fact, Lodge Cast Iron Dutch Ovens have been around for so long in so many kitchens, they might seem old-fashioned for today's cook. But if you believe the Lodge Cast Iron Dutch Oven is just a quaint relic from more traditional times—a pot for cooking chili over the campfire—think again.

The very thing that made them so valuable on the farm—their versatility—is something we can all still take advantage of. In fact, some cooks would claim it's the only pot you need. Yes, it's great for braising or slow-cooking chili, but it has so many more uses. From boiling to baking to stir-frying, cooks rely on it to produce an amazing variety of meals, from Cajun gumbo to Italian pasta to Thai curries.

Boiling and Simmering

Lodge Cast Iron Dutch Ovens excel at maintaining an even simmer without having to constantly adjust the heat under the pot. This is invaluable when making soups and stews, whether they cook for 30 or 90 minutes. And for dishes that require more heat, your Lodge Cast Iron Dutch Oven can easily reach and keep a steady boil, so you can use it for cooking pasta, blanching vegetables, or reducing sauces.

Steaming

With the addition of a steamer basket, your Lodge Cast Iron Dutch Oven can transform into a steamer. Its tight-fitting lid traps the steam and keeps the temperature constant to cook delicate vegetables, eggs, or potatoes for salad.

Frying

Whether you want to sear beef, shallow-fry chicken, or deep-fry fish fillets for a sandwich, a Lodge Cast Iron Dutch Oven can do it all. Even heating and exceptional retention mean no hot spots when searing and a steady temperature when deep frying. With a little planning, you can even stir-fry in your pot.

Braising

Of all the kitchen techniques, braising is arguably your Lodge Cast Iron Dutch Oven's greatest strength. It maintains low, even heat on the stovetop or in the oven, which results in meltingly tender meats and delectable sauces. From pork ribs cacciatore to pot roast to Moroccan chicken and sweet potatoes, you'll get perfectly delicious dinners with very little effort.

Roasting

In the oven, your sturdy pot can withstand the high heat of roasting, so it can take the place of a roasting pan, turning out beautiful meats and crisp roasted vegetables with equal ease. The radiant heat from the sides of the pot can even brown a whole chicken.

Baking

At lower oven temperatures, this versatile pot can act as a casserole dish, turning out creamy bakes with crisp brown toppings. And although it's beyond the scope of this book, you can even use it for baking desserts like apple crisp or no-knead bread.

Go Heavy Or Light

The Lodge Cast Iron Dutch Oven in most of our kitchens, whether a wedding gift, inherited from Grandma, or saved up for, is cast iron coated with enamel. It's a heavyweight vessel, both literally and figuratively. A 5- to 6-quart Lodge Cast Iron Dutch Oven will weigh 12 to 14 pounds. While this mass makes for wonderfully even cooking and heat retention, it also takes some muscle to lift. If that's not your style, there are lighter options that still provide most of the benefits of the classic cast-iron pot. The best alternative is enamel-coated cast aluminum, which weighs about 7 pounds but still gives you even heat distribution and retention. Anodized aluminum pots, usually with a nonstick interior, are another option, as are "clad" pots (stainless steel with an aluminum disk sandwiched on the bottom). Those both weigh a little less than the cast-aluminum pot, but they won't give you the even heat radiating from the sides of a heavier pot. They also heat faster than cast iron or aluminum, so you'll probably want to lower the heat on the Lodge Cast Iron Dutch Oven (oven temps can remain the same).

Keep It Clean

Most enameled Lodge Cast Iron Dutch Ovens are dishwasher safe; check the manufacturer's instructions to be sure. Anodized aluminum pots are generally not dishwasher safe; the aluminum will become discolored. Because of their large size, you may prefer to wash Lodge Cast Iron Dutch Ovens by hand with soap and a sponge or nylon kitchen scrubbie. Don't use anything abrasive like steel wool, as it can scratch the coating. For most stuck-on food, filling the pot with about an inch of hot water and letting it sit for 10 minutes will loosen the sticky bits so they can easily be scrubbed off or washed off in the dishwasher. For serious sticking, a product called Barkeeper's Friend is my go-to cleaner. Just be sure to rinse thoroughly within one minute of application and then dry (if it dries on the surface, it can dull the enamel). I also use the product occasionally when the enamel gets discolored or sticky. Le Creuset and a few other manufacturers also make enamel cleaners that will keep your enamel looking its best.

Making The Most Of Your Leftovers

A Lodge Cast Iron Dutch Oven can be ideal for making large batches of stews, soups, and braises with leftovers in mind. In fact, many of the recipes in this book taste great when reheated. Much as I love my Lodge Cast Iron Dutch Oven for this kind of cooking, I never store leftover food in the cooking pot. The heat retention that makes it so wonderful to cook with means that it also takes a long time to cool down, and that can make for unsafe food and an overworked refrigerator. Instead, transfer the food to a container with an airtight lid, or to a bowl covered with plastic wrap, and let cool on the counter to room temperature before moving it to the refrigerator.

If you're the kind of cook who likes to get creative with leftovers, a Lodge Cast Iron Dutch Oven can provide ample opportunity for improvising. You can cook a batch of chickpeas on the weekend, for instance, then use some in a salad for lunches, use another portion in a soup, and puree the rest into hummus for a delicious snack later in the week. Or cook a roast for Sunday dinner, then use the remainder of the meat for French dip sandwiches or tacos when you're pressed for time midweek.

Chapter 1: Breakfasts and Lunches

Baked Pear Oatmeal

Baked oatmeal for breakfast is like eating dessert! It will leave you happy all morning, made with good ingredients.

Preparation time and cooking time: 60 minutes | Serves: 6

Ingredients To Use:

- Nonstick cooking spray
- 2 cups old-fashioned rolled oats
- 2½ cups milk, plus more for serving
- ⅓ cup pure maple syrup, plus more for serving
- 1 egg, beaten
- ¼ teaspoon salt
- 2 medium pears, peeled, cored, and chopped

Step-by-Step Directions to cook it:

- Preheat the Lodge Cast Iron Dutch Oven to 350°F.
- Spray a pan generously with nonstick cooking spray.
- In a medium bowl, mix together the oats, milk, maple syrup, egg, salt, and pears.
- Spread the mixture evenly in the Lodge Cast Iron Dutch Oven.
- Bake uncovered for 45 to 50 minutes or until most of the liquid is absorbed and the pears are tender.
- Remove from the oven and let cool with the lid on for 5 minutes. This will loosen the oatmeal, so it doesn't stick to the pan.
- Serve topped with extra milk or maple syrup, if desired.

Nutritional value per serving: Calories: 68 kcal, Protein: 2.4g, Fat: 1.4g, Carbs: 12g

Cinnamon-Raisin Breakfast Bread Pudding

A recipe between breakfast and dessert, this simple Cinnamon-Raisin Bread Pudding is literally the best use of cinnamon-raisin bread ever.

Preparation time and cooking time: 55 minutes | Serves: 6-8

Ingredients To Use:

•¼ Cup (½ stick) unsalted butter

•4 cups whole milk

•8 large eggs

•¼ cup brown sugar

•2 teaspoons vanilla extract

•1 (1-pound) loaf cinnamon-raisin bread, cut into cubes

Step-by-Step Directions to cook it:

●Preheat your Lodge Cast Iron Dutch Oven.
●Add butter to a pot and melt in the Lodge Cast Iron Dutch Oven.
●Remove the pot from the heat and add the milk, eggs, brown sugar, and vanilla extract.
●Whisk to combine well. Stir in the cubed bread until well coated.
●Cover and return to the oven.
●Bake for about 45 minutes, until the mixture has set and is springy to the touch.
●Serve hot, sprinkled with brown sugar or maple syrup, if desired.

Nutritional value per serving: Calories: 128.1 kcal, Protein: 4.9g, Fat: 4.3g, Carbs: 18.6g

Beef Morning Quinoa

Ahh yes, quinoa again for breakfast. Doesn't it just make you want a sleepover now?

Preparation time and cooking time: 2-3 hours | Serves: 6

Ingredients To Use:

- 2 cups cooked quinoa
- 2 pounds medium roasted beef
- 3-4 slices bacon
- 1 cup cheese, shredded
- 1 large tomato, chopped
- 1 large onion, chopped
- 1 large russet potato, cubed
- 1 turnip, cubed

- ½ small green bell pepper
- ½ Anaheim pepper
- 1 teaspoon ginger, minced
- ¼ jalapeno pepper
- Cilantro, chopped
- 1 tablespoon garlic, chopped
- ¾ cup red wine vinegar
- 1 teaspoon cumin
- ½ teaspoon chili powder

Step-by-Step Directions to cook it:

1. Preheat your oven. Cut your beef into 1-2 inch cubes
2. Transfer them to your Lodge Cast Iron Dutch Oven
3. Add 2/3 of onion around beef and arrange bacon slices on top of onions
4. Add minced ginger, red wine vinegar, chopped garlic, cumin, chili powder
5. Season with salt and peppere
6. Cook on medium for about 1-2 hours until the beef is tender, add potato and turnip once the beef is almost tender
7. Once tender, remove beef from Lodge Cast Iron Dutch Oven and shred it well
8. Remove potato/turnip mixture and leave the liquid
9. Add cooked quinoa to the bottom of your pot and spread it evenly
10. Layer potato/turnip mixture on top of quinoa
11. Add shredded beef . Sprinkle shredded cheese
12. Make the pico de gallo by adding chopped tomato, pepper, and onion to a bowl and seasoning t with salt and pepper
13. Carefully place pico de gallo in the center of your dish and garnish with cilantro
14. Enjoy!

Nutritional value per serving: Calories: 600 kcal, Protein: 46g, Fat: 20g, Carbs: 50g

Perfect Mushroom Risotto

This mushroom risotto recipe, a great meatless main dish or side, is fool-proof and convenient. For a vegan main dish, a worthy and easily adapted company.

Preparation time and cooking time: 30 minutes | Serves: 6

Ingredients To Use:

• 3 tablespoons extra virgin olive oil

• 1 pound mushrooms, quartered

• 2 shallots, thinly sliced

• 1 and ¼ cups arborio rice

• 3 and ¼ cups vegetable broth, divided

• Salt as needed

• Fresh ground black pepper

• 1 cup parmesan cheese, grated

• Thinly sliced fresh chives

Step-by-Step Directions to cook it:

1. Preheat your Lodge Cast Iron Dutch Oven
2. Add 1 tablespoon oil to your pot alongside mushrooms, cook for 7-9 minutes over medium heat
3. Keep the mushrooms on the side
4. Add remaining 2 tablespoons olive oil and shallots, cook for 3 minutes over medium-high heat
5. Add rice, cook for 1 minute
6. Add half of the broth and cook for 5 minutes, simmering over medium-low heat
7. Season accordingly
8. Keep stirring until rice is tender and creamy, add remaining broth and keep stirring until the rice absorbs the broth
9. Season more
10. Once the rice is tender, add cheese and cooked mushrooms, stir to combine
11. Spoon into bowls and top with chives, enjoy!

Nutritional value per serving: Calories: 420 kcal, Protein: 22g, Fat: 20g, Carbs: 60g

Apple Pancake

Who doesn't love waking up to the aroma of a freshly cooked pancake? Add some apple, nutmeg, and cinnamon, and this Saturday morning stalwart is transformed into a sumptuous, mouthwatering treat.

Preparation time and cooking time: 40 minutes | Serves: 4-6

Ingredients To Use:

- 4 eggs
- ½ cup unbleached all-purpose flour
- ½ teaspoon baking powder
- 1 tablespoon sugar
- Pinch salt
- 1 cup milk
- 2 tablespoons unsalted butter, melted
- 1 teaspoon nutmeg
- ½ cup white sugar, divided
- ½ teaspoon ground cinnamon
- 4 tablespoons unsalted butter
- 1 large apple, peeled, cored, and sliced

Step-by-Step Directions to cook it:

1. Start heating up the oven to 425°F.
2. In a large bowl, blend the eggs, flour, baking powder, 1 tablespoon sugar, and salt. Gradually add in the milk, stirring constantly. Add the melted butter and ½ teaspoon of nutmeg. If possible, let the batter stand for 30 minutes.
3. In a small bowl, combine ¼ cup of sugar, cinnamon, and the remaining ½ teaspoon of nutmeg.
4. Melt the 4 tablespoons butter in a pot over a medium-high heat.
5. Remove the pot from the oven. Sprinkle the sugar mixture evenly over the butter, then line the bottom with the apple slices. Sprinkle the remaining ¼ cup of sugar on top.
6. Place the pot back over a medium-high heat. When the mixture begins to bubble, pour the batter evenly over the apples.
7. Cover, put in the preheated oven, and bake for 15 minutes.
8. Reduce heat to 375°F and bake for 10 minutes, or until a toothpick comes out clean. Use a plastic spatula to loosen the pancake, slide it onto a serving platter, cut into wedges, and serve.

Nutritional value per serving: Calories: 120.8 kcal, Protein: 8.6g, Fat: 1.2g, Carbs: 18.7g

Country Fair Omelet

The addition of sausage transforms a light omelet into hearty fare that will satiate the entire family—and keep them energized for all the weekend chores. For a tasty twist, swap in breakfast sausage made with a blend of pork and beef, or try chicken links for a lighter, healthier option.

Preparation time and cooking time: 40 minutes | Serves: 6-8

Ingredients To Use:

- •2 tablespoons olive, coconut, or canola oil, or cooking spray
- •½ pound breakfast sausage, cut crosswise into 1/4-inch-thick slices
- •½ pound bacon, thickly sliced
- •½ onion, diced
- •1 clove garlic, minced
- •1 red bell pepper, seeded and chopped
- •1 cup mushrooms, chopped
- •9 eggs
- •½ cup milk
- •1 cup grated Cheddar cheese
- •Salt
- •Freshly ground black pepper

Step-by-Step Directions to cook it:

1. Preheat the oven to 375°F.
2. Heat a pot over medium heat. Add the oil or a spritz of cooking spray, and fry the sausage until browned, then remove and set aside on a plate, using a paper towel to absorb any excess fat.
3. Fry the bacon until browned, and drain excess fat from the pot.
4. Add the sausage, onion, garlic, pepper, and mushrooms. Sauté until the vegetables are tender.
5. In a bowl, mix the eggs and milk, then pour the egg mixture into the pot.
6. Cover, put in the preheated oven, and bake for 20 minutes, or until the eggs are firm.
7. Sprinkle cheese on top, and season with salt and pepper. Return the pot to the oven for a few minutes, uncovered, until the cheese melts. Serve.

Nutritional value per serving: Calories: 720 kcal, Protein: 25g, Fat: 46g, Carbs: 51g

Baked Eggs with Creamy Polenta

With minimal prep time, this is the perfect brunch to whip together when entertaining overnight guests. Let the hard-working Lodge Cast Iron Dutch Oven do most of the work while you sit back and catch up with friends and family over a hot cup of joe.

Preparation time and cooking time: 50 minutes | Serves: 4-6

Ingredients To Use:

- ½ cup instant polenta
- 1 cup water
- 1 cup milk
- ½ cup finely grated pecorino romano cheese
- Pinch salt
- Pinch of black pepper
- 4 eggs

Step-by-Step Directions to cook it:

1. Start heating up the oven to 375°F.
2. Generously coat a pot with cooking spray. Add the polenta, water, milk, cheese, salt, and pepper. Stir.
3. Cover, put in the preheated oven, and bake for 30 to 35 minutes, stirring once halfway through, until polenta is tender.
4. Use the back of a spoon to make four deep wells in the polenta, then crack an egg into each well. Cover the pot and bake for 10 to 12 minutes, or until the egg whites are cooked.

Nutritional value per serving: Calories: 229 kcal, Protein: 14.3g, Fat: 10.5g, Carbs: 19g

PB&J Pockets

This is a delicious Lodge Cast Iron Dutch Oven take on the classic PB&J. Sure to satisfy kids of all ages, this recipe provides the perfect indoor activity to entertain the troops on a rain-soaked Sunday morning. They'll love rolling up their sleeves and joining in the prep work!

Preparation time and cooking time: 16 minutes | Serves: 2

Ingredients To Use:

- 2 slices 1-inch-thick white bread
- 2 tablespoons peanut butter
- 2 tablespoons jam (choice of strawberry, raspberry, blackberry, or blueberry)
- 2 eggs, lightly beaten
- 2 tablespoons milk
- 1 teaspoon maple syrup
- ¼ teaspoon vanilla extract
- Pinch nutmeg
- Extra-virgin olive oil

For The Toppings

- Your choice of crème fraîche, honey, fresh berries, or pancake syrup

Step-by-Step Directions to cook it:

1. Preheat your Lodge Cast Iron Dutch Oven.
2. Use a serrated knife to carefully cut horizontally through each slice of bread to within ¼ inch of the bottom crust, creating a pocket. Be careful not to cut through the crust.
3. Spread a layer of peanut butter and a layer of jam in each pocket, and set the bread aside.
4. In a medium bowl, combine the eggs, milk, maple syrup, vanilla extract, and nutmeg, and whisk until well combined.
5. Lightly oil the pot. Dip a slice of stuffed bread into the egg batter, covering both sides. Place the bread into the pot and fry for 2 to 3 minutes, or until golden brown. Turn the bread over and fry the other side. Repeat as needed.
6. Serve 2 slices with a choice of toppings.

Nutritional value per serving: Calories: 230 kcal, Protein: 0.5g, Fat: 7g, Carbs: 70g

Breakfast Ratatouille With Chorizo, Eggs & Cheese

Though it's intended here as part of a breakfast dish, the simple but tasty vegetable and chorizo sauce is extremely versatile—make extra and save it for when you need a delicious accompaniment to a pasta dish in a pinch. Store in a large mason jar in the refrigerator or in plastic bags in the freezer.

Preparation time and cooking time: 60 minutes | Serves: 4-6

Ingredients To Use:

- 2 tablespoons extra-virgin olive oil
- 5½ ounces chorizo, diced
- 2 red onions, chopped
- 3 garlic cloves, minced
- 1 zucchini, diced
- 1½ pounds portobello mushrooms
- 2 red bell peppers, seeded and diced
- 1 (15-ounce) can chopped tomatoes
- 2 tablespoons white wine vinegar
- 1¼ cups water, plus more if necessary
- 1 teaspoon sugar
- Salt
- Freshly ground black pepper
- 4 eggs
- 5 ounces Parmesan cheese, grated

Step-by-Step Directions to cook it:

1. Preheat the oven to 400°F.
2. Heat the olive oil in a pot over medium heat. Add the chorizo, onions, and garlic, and cook for 4 to 5 minutes.
3. Add the zucchini, mushrooms, and peppers, and cook for 2 to 3 minutes, stirring occasionally.
4. Add the can of tomatoes, stir in the vinegar, water, and sugar, and season with salt and pepper. Boil, then reduce heat to a low simmer. Cook for 25 to 30 minutes, stirring occasionally. If the sauce becomes too thick, add more water.
5. Make 4 deep wells in the mixture with the back of a spoon. Crack an egg into each well. Sprinkle cheese on top. Bake for 10 to 12 minutes, or until the sauce is bubbling and the eggs have set.

Nutritional value per serving: Calories: 330 kcal, Protein: 13g, Fat: 21g, Carbs: 20g

Ham & Potatoes Au Gratin

If you end up with leftovers, serve this au gratin dish for a delicious teatime treat. It makes a satisfying savory topping on a thick wedge of Texas toast.

Preparation time and cooking time: 35 minutes | Serves: 4-6

Ingredients To Use:

- 4 tablespoons butter
- 1 onion, minced
- 2 cups milk
- 3 tablespoons flour
- 1½ cups diced cooked ham
- 3 cups diced potatoes
- Salt
- Freshly ground black pepper
- ½ cup grated Cheddar cheese

Step-by-Step Directions to cook it:

1. Preheat the oven to 400°F.
2. Start melting the butter in a pot over medium heat. Sauté the onion, add the milk, and stir.
3. Gradually blend in the flour, stirring constantly, until the mixture thickens.
4. Add the ham and potatoes, and mix well. Season with salt and pepper, and sprinkle the cheese on top.
5. Cover, put in the preheated oven, and bake for 20 minutes.

Nutritional value per serving: Calories: 181.6 kcal, Protein: 13.2g, Fat: 4.1g, Carbs: 23.2g

Scrambled Breakfast Hash

This decadent dish makes a fantastic post-holiday breakfast. In place of the sausages called for here, simply use the leftover meat from your celebrations in this delicious hash. Try ham, turkey, kielbasa, brisket, or anything else you might have on hand— even baked or smoked salmon. This recipe also works wonderfully well with meat substitutes like seasoned tofu or veggie crumbles.

Preparation time and cooking time: 2 hours & 40 minutes | Serves: 6

Ingredients To Use:

- 2 tablespoons extra-virgin olive oil
- 1 pound breakfast sausages, diced
- 4 medium Yukon Gold potatoes, chopped
- 8 ounces mushrooms, sliced
- 1 onion, chopped
- Salt
- Freshly ground black pepper
- 6 eggs
- 3 tablespoons milk
- ½ cup shredded cheese (Cheddar or Monterey Jack)
- Salsa or hot pepper sauce, for garnish

Step-by-Step Directions to cook it:

1. Preheat the oven to 325°F.
2. Heat the olive oil in a pot over medium-high heat, and cook the sausages until browned. Drain off the fat. Add the potatoes, mushrooms, and onion, season with salt and pepper, and gently stir. Cover, put in the preheated oven, and bake for 1½ to 2 hours, or until the potatoes are tender.
3. In a medium bowl, whisk together the eggs and milk. Pour the egg mixture over the potato mixture. Sprinkle the cheese on top. Cover and bake for 10 to 15 minutes, or until the eggs are set and the cheese has melted.
4. Garnish with the salsa or hot pepper sauce.

Nutritional value per serving: Calories: 210 kcal, Protein: 15g, Fat: 9g, Carbs: 18g

Ham, Cheese & Potato Bake

If you don't have English muffins on hand, use any type of toasted bread. If using large slices of bread, cut in half for adults and into soldiers (thin strips of toast) for children's plates. This dish easily becomes gluten-sensitivity-friendly by substituting gluten-free bread.

Preparation time and cooking time: 2 hours & 10 minutes | Serves: 8

Ingredients To Use:

- 4 cups frozen diced hash brown potatoes
- 8 ounces cooked ham, chopped
- 1 cup shredded Muenster cheese
- 1 red bell pepper, chopped
- 1 onion, chopped
- 6 eggs, lightly beaten
- 1 (15-ounce) can condensed cream of mushroom soup
- ½ cup milk
- Salt
- Freshly ground black pepper
- 8 English muffins, split and toasted

Step-by-Step Directions to cook it:

1. Preheat the Lodge Cast Iron Dutch Oven to 325°F.
2. In a pot coated with cooking spray, combine the potatoes, ham, cheese, red pepper, and onion.
3. In a medium bowl, mix the eggs, soup, and milk. Season with salt and black pepper, then pour the egg mixture over the potato mixture.
4. Cover, put in the preheated oven, and bake for 1½ to 2 hours.
5. Serve over freshly toasted English muffins.

Nutritional value per serving: Calories: 206 kcal, Protein: 6g, Fat: 10.1g, Carbs: 22.7g

Chapter 2: Beef, Pork & Lamb Recipes

Lodge Cast Iron Dutch Oven Beef Roast

Lodge Cast Iron Dutch Oven pot roast right from the oven with carrots and potatoes becomes juicy and fork tender.

Preparation time and cooking time: 2 hours & 25 minutes | Serves: 4

Ingredients To Use:

- Salt and pepper as needed
- Cooking fat such as butter or ghee
- Fresh thyme sprigs
- 2 bay leaves
- 2 cups beef stock
- ½ cup red wine, optional

- 1 tablespoon tomato paste
- 3 cloves garlic, minced
- 2 onions, quartered
- 1 celeriac, diced
- 4 sweet potatoes, cut up into chunks
- 3 carrots, peeled and sliced
- 4-5 pounds beef roast, bottom round

Step-by-Step Directions to cook it:

1. Start heating your oven to a temperature of 350 degrees F
2. Season your beef generously with salt and pepper
3. Take your pan and place it over medium-high heat
4. Add butter/ghee and let it melt
5. Add your roast and brown all sides, for about 1-2 minutes each side
6. Add garlic, onion, tomato paste and cook for 2-3 minutes
7. Add wine if you are using and scrap the bottom of your pan
8. Lower heat and let it simmer until halved
9. Add remaining vegetables, thyme, stock and bay leaves
10. Bring the mix to a simmer (covered)
11. Transfer to oven and roast for about 2 hours until the thickest part of the meat reaches 145 degrees F
12. Let it cool, carve and enjoy!

Nutritional value per serving: Calories: 1460 kcal, Protein: 184g, Fat: 47g, Carbs: 57g

Single Pot Beef Lasagna

SO VERY Large are the feelings I have for this Super Simple recipe, often referred to as Pot o 'Saucy Noodles with Cheese-Melted Goodness.

Preparation time and cooking time: 1 hour & 20 minutes | Serves: 4

Ingredients To Use:

- 6-8 slices bacon, cut up into small pieces
- 3 carrots, minced
- 3 shallots, minced
- 1 pound beef, ground
- Salt and pepper to taste
- 1 jar (25 ounces) tomato basil sauce
- ½ cup dry red wine
- 4 ounces cream cheese
- 6-8 ounces fresh mozzarella cheese
- 4 ounces whole-wheat no-boil lasagna noodles
- Basil and parmesan cheese, for topping

Step-by-Step Directions to cook it:

1. Start heating your oven to a temperature of 350 degrees F
2. Take a large ovenproof skillet and brown your bacon until it is crispy
3. Add carrots and shallots, Saute for 5 minutes until tender and fragrant
4. Add your ground beef and season it with salt and pepper, brown until no longer pink
5. Drain any excess grease
6. Add tomato sauce, wine, and meat to skillet
7. Simmer for about 10 minutes over medium-low heat
8. Stir in cream cheese and simmer until melted
9. Break each lasagna noodles into 3-4 pieces and stir them into the meat mixture until fully covered in sauce
10. Lay your noodles flat in the pan
11. Tuck few slices of fresh cheese underneath and between the noodles
12. Place remaining slices of fresh mozzarella cheese on top. Bake for about 25 minutes. You have the option to brown your cheese, in that case, you have to heat your oven to 425 degrees F and cook for 10 minutes more
13. Let it sit for few minutes and top with parmesan and basil. Enjoy!

Nutritional value per serving: Calories: 704 kcal, Protein: 43g, Fat: 32g, Carbs: 57g

Peppercorn Pork Chops

One of my favorites is this simple pork chop recipe. The Peppercorn Sauce is perfect for plate-licking, and the chops are fantastic.

Preparation time and cooking time: 30 minutes | Serves: 4

Ingredients To Use:

- •4 (8-10 ounces) each, pork chops, 1 inch thick at room temp
- •1 tablespoon coarsely crushed black peppercorns
- •2 tablespoons extra virgin olive oil
- •1 (16 ounces) bag frozen French-style green beans
- •Salt and pepper to taste

Step-by-Step Directions to cook it:

1. Preheat your Lodge Cast Iron Dutch Oven.
2. Pat chops dry using a paper towel, rub each chop on both sides with peppercorns and press hard
3. Set your pan over medium heat and add olive oil, let it heat up
4. Add pork chops and cook for 6-8 minutes each side, remove heat and let them rest for 5 minutes before transferring to a plate
5. Add green beans to oven and cook for 5 minutes over medium-high heat, season with salt and pepper
6. Serve and enjoy!

Nutritional value per serving: Calories: 315 kcal, Protein: 37g, Fat: 15g, Carbs: 8g

French Onion Pork Chops

Tired of making the same old techniques for chicken? Maybe try pork instead! All the wonderful flavours of French onion soup are in these smothered pork chops.

Preparation time and cooking time: 60 minutes | Serves: 4

Ingredients To Use:

- •4 bone-in pork chops
- •1 tablespoon butter
- •1 cup red onion, sliced
- •1 can condensed cream, mushroom soup
- •1 cup sour cream
- •¼ cup red wine
- •1 pack dried French onion soup mix

Step-by-Step Directions to cook it:

1. Prepare your Lodge Cast Iron Dutch Oven
2. Add butter and pork chops and cook for 5 minutes before turning
3. Add onions, cook for 3 minutes
4. Take a bowl and add cream mushroom soup, sour cream, wine, French onion soup mix
5. Pour mixture over pork chops
6. Cover and cook for 45 minutes until fully cooked
7. Enjoy!

Nutritional value per serving: Calories: 553 kcal, Protein: 37g, Fat: 20g, Carbs: 56g

Pork Sausage And Cider Braised Onions, Cabbage

Put together the hearty elements for a great winter recipe.

Preparation time and cooking time: 60 minutes | Serves: 4

Ingredients To Use:

- 1 and ½ pounds smoked pork sausage, sliced

- 1 cup yellow onions, sliced

- 1 cup granny smith apple, diced

- 4 cups cabbage, shredded

- 1 cup apple cider

- 1 teaspoon ground ginger

- 1 teaspoon salt

- 1 teaspoon pepper

Step-by-Step Directions to cook it:

1. Preheat your Lodge Cast Iron Dutch Oven
2. Add pork sausage, onions, and apples
3. Toss well and cook for 5-7 minutes
4. Add cabbage, apple cider, ground ginger, salt and pepper
5. Toss well and cook for 35-40 minutes Until sausage and cabbages are finely cooked
6. Serve and enjoy!

Nutritional value per serving: Calories: 214 kcal, Protein: 11g, Fat: 17g, Carbs: 6g

Country Pork Ragu

You've still never tried the best pasta sauce: hearty, meaty, deeply seasoned pork ragu.

Preparation time and cooking time: 2 hours & 45 minutes | Serves: 4

Ingredients To Use:

- •1 tablespoon extra-virgin olive oil
- •2-3 pounds boneless country-style pork ribs
- •1 teaspoon seasoned salt
- •½ teaspoon fresh ground black pepper
- •3 garlic cloves, chopped
- •½ cup red wine
- •1 (28 ounces0 can crushed tomatoes, with basil and oregano

Step-by-Step Directions to cook it:

1. Pre-heat your Lodge Cast Iron Dutch Oven to 325 degrees F
2. Take a large pan place it over medium heat
3. Put the olive oil and let it heat up, season ribs and add them, brown for 5 minutes per side
4. Transfer to a plate
5. Add garlic to the pot and cook for 2 minutes, deglaze with wine
6. Add tomatoes, return ribs to the pot
7. Bake in the oven for 2 to 2 ½ hours until meat starts falling apart
8. Shred meat using two forks and discard bones, mix in shredded meat with gravy
9. Season with salt and pepper
10. Serve and enjoy over pasta!

Nutritional value per serving: Calories: 342 kcal, Protein: 20g, Fat: 23g, Carbs: 12g

Pot Roast

Once a Pot Roast has been cooked to perfection, it will be tender and pull apart easily. It is an extremely versatile cooked meat: the leftovers make great Poor Boy sandwiches the next day, or even beef tacos.

Preparation time and cooking time: 2 hours and 10 minutes | Serves: 4-6

Ingredients To Use:

- •2 tablespoons olive oil

- •1 medium chuck roast, about 2 inches thick

- •1/4 cup red wine vinegar

- •1 onion, quartered

- •2 garlic cloves, quartered

- •Salt, to taste

- •Pepper, to taste

- •Fresh or Dried Rosemary

Step-by-Step Directions to cook it:

1. Preheat your Dutch ven

2. Sprinkle roast with vinegar, salt and pepper, and herbs, and let marinate overnight.

3. Put olive oil into bottom of your pot.

4. Add roast, sprinkle with onion and garlic, and cover pot.

5. Put to bake slowly at 325°F for two hours.

6. Check roast occasionally to prevent burning.

Nutritional value per serving: Calories: 87 kcal, Protein: 5.6g, Fat: 6.1g, Carbs: 2.3g

Mamma Mia! Beef Meatballs in Tomato Sauce

Everybody has their own secret meatball recipe, which goes to show that there are infinite ways to make a good meatball.

Preparation time and cooking time: 50 minutes | Serves: 4-6

Ingredients To Use:

- 1 tablespoon olive oil
- 6 cloves garlic, minced fine
- 1 lb. ground beef
- Herbs de Provence
- 1 cup minced parsley
- 2 tablespoons tomato paste
- 1/2 cup dry bread crumbs
- Dash of chili powder
- Salt, to taste
- Pepper, to taste
- 2 cups tomatoes, chopped
- 1 cup tomato sauce
- 1 cup broth
- 1/2 cup red wine

Step-by-Step Directions to cook it:

1. Preheat your Lodge Cast Iron Dutch Oven
2. Put aside 2 garlic cloves, minced, for later.
3. Mix remaining garlic, meat, herbs, parsley, 2 spoons tomato paste, bread crumbs, and spices in a bowl. Shape into golf ball sized meatballs.
4. Put olive oil into a pot.
5. Heat oil for 30 seconds on medium heat, then add meatballs and brown evenly on all sides. Do not cook completely.
6. Add tomato sauce mixed with remaining garlic, beef or vegetable broth and chopped tomatoes, and red wine, and simmer for 20 minutes on low heat, covered.
7. Add salt and pepper to taste.
8. Serve over pasta, or any other way you want to eat it.

Nutritional value per serving: Calories: 252 kcal, Protein: 26.8g, Fat: 8.1g, Carbs: 14.4g

Beef Stew with Fresh Herbs

Beef stew is always a very comforting food on a cold night. Paired with a bottle of red wine and crusty bread it is a highly satisfying meal.

Preparation time and cooking time: 2 hours and 15 minutes | Serves: 4-6

Ingredients To Use:

- 2 tablespoons olive oil
- 6 cloves garlic, quartered
- 1 onion, chopped fine
- 2 lbs. beef stew chunks
- 1 large leek, chopped
- 2 carrots, chopped
- 2 cups mushrooms, chopped
- 2 cups tomatoes, chopped

- 4 potatoes, peeled and quartered
- 2 tablespoons dried Herbes de Provence.
- Salt, to taste
- Pepper, to taste
- Chopped parsley, for garnish
- 1 cup of red wine or 1/4 cup sherry
- 4 cups of beef broth, or vegetable broth
- Extra hot water as needed

Step-by-Step Directions to cook it:

1. Prepare your oven. Heat oil for 30 seconds on medium heat, then add chopped garlic, chopped onion and cook until beginning to get translucent. Stir every two minutes to prevent burning.
2. Add meat chunks and brown slightly, mixing often.
3. Add your chopped vegetables in the following order, stirring between each addition: mushrooms, tomatoes, carrots, potatoes.
4. Add broth and wine, then fresh herbs. Make sure to cover meat and vegetables with enough liquid. If more is needed, add hot water as necessary. This liquid should evaporate somewhat. Mixture shouldn't be too soupy, but not too dry either.
5. Simmer slowly, 90 minutes to 2 hours. Meat will be very tender when ready.
6. Make sure to remove any large sticks from the fresh herbs.
7. Salt to taste before serving.
8. Add parsley garnish.

Nutritional value per serving: Calories: 529 kcal, Protein: 25.4g, Fat: 27.9g, Carbs: 44.8g

Beef Goulash

A slow-cooked roast melts in your mouth, especially when paired with the fragrant spice and flavors of paprika and tomatoes. Enjoy with lots of sour cream!

Preparation time and cooking time: 3 hours and 15 minutes | Serves: 4-6

Ingredients To Use:

- •2 tablespoons olive oil
- •2 to 3 lbs. chuck roast
- •2 onions, quartered
- •4 garlic cloves, crushed
- •1 cup tomato sauce
- •2 cups tomatoes, chopped
- •Salt, to taste
- •1 tablespoon paprika
- •Handful of fresh herbs: tarragon, rosemary, thyme

Step-by-Step Directions to cook it:

1. Prepare your oven. Heat oil for 30 seconds on medium heat, then add garlic and onions and stir. Cover and continue to cook on medium heat for 5-6 minutes, until beginning to get translucent. Stir every two minutes to prevent burning.
2. Place beef in mixture, and pour tomato sauce over it.
3. Add salt and paprika.
4. Cover with chopped tomato and fresh herbs.
5. Cover and bake at 275°F for 3 hours.
6. Meat should be tender and come apart easily with fork.
7. Serve with sour cream and boiled potatoes.

Nutritional value per serving: Calories: 408 kcal, Protein: 51.7g, Fat: 17.6g, Carbs: 9.3g

Hungarian Goulash

Goulash is a thick soup, or thin stew depending on whom you ask, that is flavored with Hungarian paprika. Serve goulash over rice or egg noodles with extra sour cream.

Preparation time and cooking time: 2 hours and 45 minutes | Serves: 8

Ingredients To Use:

- 1/4 cup all-purpose flour
- 1/4 teaspoon salt
- 3 pounds chuck roast, cut into 2" cubes
- 1/4 cup vegetable oil, divided
- 2 large onions, peeled and sliced
- 2 cloves garlic, peeled and minced
- 1/4 cup Hungarian sweet paprika
- 4 tablespoons tomato paste
- 2 cups beef broth
- Water, to cover beef
- 1/2 cup sour cream, for garnish

Step-by-Step Directions to cook it:

1. In a large zip-top bag combine flour and salt. Add cubed beef and toss to coat.
2. Set your Lodge Cast Iron Dutch Oven to medium heat and add 1 tablespoon oil. Brown beef on all sides in two batches, adding more oil between batches, and making sure not to crowd the pan, about 5–8 minutes per batch. Start transferring the browned beef to a plate and set aside.
3. Add remaining 2 tablespoons of oil to the pan along with onion. Cook until onion is soft, about 5 minutes, then add garlic, paprika, and tomato paste. Cook until spices and tomato paste have browned slightly, about 5 minutes. Return beef to the pan and coat beef with the onions and paprika.
4. Add beef broth to the pan and, with a wooden spoon or heatproof spatula, scrape any browned bits off the bottom of the Lodge Cast Iron Dutch Oven. Add enough water to just cover beef and bring mixture to a boil. Once it reaches a boil reduce heat to low, cover with the lid, and simmer 2 hours or until the meat is fork tender. Serve the goulash with dollops of sour cream.

Nutritional value per serving: Calories: 278.8 kcal, Protein: 35.2 g, Fat: 6.1 g, Carbs: 15.5 g

Chapter 3: Fish & Seafood Recipes

Spice-Rubbed Salmon

To round out this delectable dish, serve on a bed of greens (butter lettuce is a mild option, or watercress lends a peppery kick). Drizzle the greens with lemon juice and olive oil, and season with salt and pepper.

Preparation time and cooking time: 30 minutes | Serves: 6

Ingredients To Use:

• 1 teaspoon kosher salt

• 1 teaspoon chili powder

• 1 teaspoon cumin

• 4 (6-ounce) salmon fillets, skin on

• 1 tablespoon extra-virgin olive oil

Step-by-Step Directions to cook it:

1. Preheat the oven to 375°F.
2. In a small bowl, combine the salt, chili powder, and cumin. Rub the salmon fillets with the spice mixture, coating them evenly.
3. Heat the olive oil in the Lodge Cast Iron Dutch Oven set to medium-high heat. Place the salmon fillets in the pot, skin-side up. Cook for 3 minutes, or until the tops are evenly browned. For medium-rare, flip and cook for 3 minutes. For medium to well-done, Cover, put in the preheated oven, and bake for 5 to 10 minutes.

Nutritional value per serving: Calories: 323 kcal, Protein: 23g, Fat: 19g, Carbs: 15g

Steamed Mussels With Bacon

Mussels are not only quick to prepare, they're also inexpensive, readily available, and deliciously elegant. Mussels are sold and cooked live. Although they can live out of water for a few days, they should be kept well chilled.

Preparation time and cooking time: 25 minutes | Serves: 6

Ingredients To Use:

- 2 to 3 tablespoons extra-virgin olive oil, plus more for garnish
- ½ cup bacon, diced
- 4 cloves garlic, thinly sliced
- 1 onion, chopped
- 1 cup dry white wine
- 2 teaspoons paprika
- 2 dozen mussels, cleaned and beards removed
- Cayenne pepper, for garnish
- Handful fresh oregano, chopped, for garnish

Step-by-Step Directions to cook it:

1. In the medium heated Lodge Cast Iron Dutch Oven, place the olive oil and cook the bacon. Once the bacon fat begins to render, 2 minutes, add the garlic and onion. Cook, stirring, until they are translucent.
2. Add the wine and stir in the paprika.
3. Add the mussels. Increase the heat to high, and cook for about 30 seconds, or until the alcohol has evaporated.
4. Reduce the heat to medium-low. Cover and steam for 5 to 8 minutes, until all the mussels have opened. Discard any mussels that haven't opened.
5. Garnish with a drizzle of olive oil, a sprinkle of cayenne pepper, and chopped oregano.

Nutritional value per serving: Calories: 890 kcal, Protein: 57g, Fat: 53g, Carbs: 27g

Spanish Paella

Like so many other popular recipes, paella was originally a peasant dish made with whatever ingredients were available and cooked in a pot over an open fire—which makes it a perfect dish for a Lodge Cast Iron Dutch Oven.

Preparation time and cooking time: 40 minutes | Serves: 4

Ingredients To Use:

•½ cup of cheese preferably shredded

•¼ teaspoon of Italian seasoning

•1 lb ground beef

•1 egg

Taco seasoning

•½ teaspoon of smoked paprika

•1 teaspoon of ground cumin

•½ teaspoon of garlic powder

•¼ teaspoon of onion powder

•1 teaspoon of chili powder

•¼ teaspoon of salt

•½ teaspoon of cocoa powder

Step-by-Step Directions to cook it:

1.Simmer the ground beef for about 20 minutes, then add all the taco seasoning.

2.Set the waffle-maker and preheat it. Whisk the eggs in a bowl and add the shredded cheese and Italian seasoning. Mix until well-combined.

3.Pour the mixture into the waffle-maker and allow it to cook for 4 minutes. Repeat the process until the batter is finished.

4.Fold the chaffle and place a piece of taco beef between the sides. You can top it with sliced tomatoes, cheese, and lettuce (optional).

5.Serve immediately.

Nutritional value per serving: Calories: 355 kcal, Protein: 6.3g, Fat: 0.8g, Carbs: 78.9g

Grilled Swordfish Steaks

Firm fish steaks cook quickly, and make a delicious and super healthy protein alternative. For an appetizing light lunch or supper, serve with avocado slices and your favorite salsa, and garnish with a wedge of lime.

Preparation time and cooking time: 20 minutes | Serves: 4

Ingredients To Use:

- 4 tablespoons extra-virgin olive oil, divided
- 2 teaspoons chili powder
- 2 teaspoons dried oregano, crumbled
- 1 teaspoon sea salt
- ½ teaspoon freshly ground black pepper
- 4 swordfish steaks, cut ¾-inch thick

Step-by-Step Directions to cook it:

1. Mix 3 tablespoons of olive oil with the chili powder, oregano, salt, and pepper. Brush the swordfish steaks with the oil mixture.
2. In the medium heated Lodge Cast Iron Dutch Oven, place the remaining 1 tablespoon of olive oil. Add the swordfish steaks and cook for about 4 minutes. Turn and cook for a few minutes, until browned on both sides but still moist. It's best if the fish is slightly undercooked in the center, as it will continue to cook a bit after you've removed it from the heat.

Nutritional value per serving: Calories: 226.9 kcal, Protein: 23g, Fat: 11.3g, Carbs: 1g

Linguine With Clams

If you're looking for an easy meal guaranteed to impress, clams fit the bill perfectly. Cooks of all skill levels can prepare these tasty mollusks with confidence.

Preparation time and cooking time: 50 minutes | Serves: 8

Ingredients To Use:

•2 (16-ounce) packages linguine

•2 tablespoons extra-virgin olive oil, divided

•4 cloves garlic, minced

•3 (28-ounce) cans plum tomatoes

•4 teaspoons sugar

•Salt

•Freshly ground black pepper

•2 pounds littleneck clams, cleaned

•Fresh basil leaves, torn, for garnish

Step-by-Step Directions to cook it:

1. In a Lodge Cast Iron Dutch Oven, cook the linguine according to the directions on the package. Drain and set aside.
2. In the same oven, heat 1 tablespoon of olive oil over medium heat. Add the garlic and cook for 1 minute. Stir in the tomatoes, the sugar, and the remaining olive oil. Lower the heat and simmer for 20 minutes, stirring frequently. Season with salt and pepper.
3. Add the clams. Cook for 5 minutes, or until the clams open. Discard any that don't. Stir in the linguine and toss to coat. Garnish with the basil.

Nutritional value per serving: Calories: 175 kcal, Protein: 15.6 g, Fat: 2.5g, Carbs: 19g

Salmon With Spinach

Salmon needs little in the way of embellishment. Just make sure not to overcook it— it should be just barely cooked in the center when the pot is removed from the oven. Wild-caught salmon is a cook's treasure, but farm-raised will do very nicely, too.

Preparation time and cooking time: 25 minutes | Serves: 6

Ingredients To Use:

• 3 tablespoons unsalted butter

• 2 pounds fresh baby spinach

• 4 shallots, minced

• 6 salmon fillets

• 3 tablespoons fresh lemon juice

• Sea salt

• Freshly ground black pepper

• 2 teaspoons finely chopped fresh rosemary leaves

• 6 lemon wedges, for garnish

• Horseradish cream sauce, for garnish

Step-by-Step Directions to cook it:

1. Preheat the oven to 325°F.
2. Coat the bottom of a pan or pot, with the butter. Spread the spinach leaves evenly over the butter, and sprinkle with the minced shallots. Place the salmon fillets on the spinach, skin-side down, and drizzle with the lemon juice. Season with the salt, pepper, and rosemary.
3. Cover, put in the preheated oven, and bake for 8 to 10 minutes. Uncover the pot and check the fish for doneness. If needed, finish the cooking with the pot uncovered for 3 to 5 minutes, or until the fish is opaque and the salmon flakes. Garnish with lemon wedges or a dollop of horseradish sauce.

Nutritional value per serving: Calories: 559 kcal, Protein: 64g, Fat: 29.7g, Carbs: 7g

Grouper With Vegetables

Grouper is a lean, firm, white-fleshed fish with a meaty texture and a flavor so mild and subtle, it appeals to even the pickiest palates. Though supply peaks in the warm months, from April to October, it's available all year round. This delicious one-pot dish is low in calories.

Preparation time and cooking time: 1 hour & 10 minutes | Serves: 4-6

Ingredients To Use:

- 2 pounds grouper
- 2 tablespoons extra-virgin olive oil
- 1 fennel bulb, thinly sliced
- 2 celery stalks, thinly sliced
- 6 shallots, skinned and chopped
- Salt
- Freshly ground black pepper
- 4 ounces butter, cut into small chunks
- 2 teaspoons chopped fresh dill

Step-by-Step Directions to cook it:

1. Remove the fine membrane covering the grouper. Remove the central bone (if the fish is not already deboned), and cut the fish into 1½-inch-thick diagonal slices.
2. Let your Lodge Cast Iron Dutch Oven become medium heated. Place olive oil in a pot and transfer to the oven. Add the fennel, celery, and shallots, and cook until they begin to soften. Transfer to a small bowl.
3. Brown the fish in the oil and transfer to a plate. Return the vegetables to the pot, then lay the fish on top. Season with salt and pepper.
4. Cover and cook over a low heat for 5 minutes. Transfer the vegetables to a serving platter, and cover to keep warm. Cover the Lodge Cast Iron Dutch Oven, and cook the fish for 30 to 40 minutes, or until tender.
5. Transfer the fish to the serving platter with the vegetables.
6. Place back over the heat. Return the liquid to a boil, and stir in the butter. Add the dill and cook, stirring until thickened. Season with salt and pepper, and pour the butter sauce over the fish.

Nutritional value per serving: Calories: 196.7 kcal, Protein: 24.2g, Fat: 8.6g, Carbs: 5.9g

Bouillabaisse

Bouillabaisse originated in the French seaport of Marseille, where the local fishermen made a stew from the bony rockfish they weren't able to sell to restaurants or markets.

Preparation time and cooking time: 4 hours and 30 minutes | Serves: 4-6

Ingredients To Use:

- 3 tablespoons extra-virgin olive oil
- 6 garlic cloves, minced
- 1 to 2 onions (about ¾ pound), diced
- 1 shallot, minced
- 1 celery stalk, minced
- 1 carrot, diced
- 1½ tablespoons tomato paste
- ½ teaspoon saffron
- 1 teaspoon minced basil or 1 fresh basil leaf
- 2 tablespoons minced fresh parsley
- Salt
- Freshly ground black pepper 1 (28-ounce) can diced tomatoes, undrained
- 2 cups clam juice
- 1 (8-ounce) jar fresh oysters, juice reserved
- 1 pound whitefish (cod, halibut, or trout), cut into bite-size pieces
- 2½ pounds seafood mix (shrimp, clams, mussels, lobsters, scallops, crabmeat, or squid)
- 2 tablespoons chopped fresh parsley, for garnish

Step-by-Step Directions to cook it:

1. In the medium heated Lodge Cast Iron Dutch Oven, set in a pod and add the olive oil. Add the garlic, onion, shallot, celery, and carrot, and sauté until lightly golden, about 20 minutes.
2. Add the tomato paste, saffron, basil, minced parsley, salt, and pepper. Mix well.
3. Add the tomatoes, clam juice, and juice from the jar of oysters. Bring the pot to a boil, lower the heat, and simmer for 15 minutes.
4. Add the oysters, whitefish, and seafood mix. Bring the pot back to a boil. Skim off any scum or fat. Lower the heat and simmer for 15 minutes.
5. Garnish with the chopped parsley.

Nutritional value per serving: Calories: 241 kcal, Protein: 33.55 g, Fat: 8.88g, Carbs: 4.63g

Teriyaki-Glazed Salmon with Asparagus

This salmon gets marinated in a sweet and tangy teriyaki sauce, then roasted in the Lodge Cast Iron Dutch Oven with fresh asparagus. The rich fish is complemented by the delicious sauce, and the asparagus adds brightness and color to the dish.

Preparation time and cooking time: 40 minutes | Serves: 4

Ingredients To Use:

•4 (6-ounce) salmon fillets

•⅓ cup teriyaki sauce or Asian stir-fry sauce (store-bought or homemade)

•1 pound asparagus, trimmed

•2 tablespoons extra-virgin olive oil

•1 teaspoon salt

•1 tablespoon sesame seeds

•2 scallions, white and green parts, chopped

Step-by-Step Directions to cook it:

1.Place the salmon in a shallow dish, and pour the teriyaki sauce over it. Cover and refrigerate for 20 minutes.
2.Preheat the oven to 400°F.
3.In a pot, toss the asparagus with the olive oil and salt. Discard the teriyaki marinade, and place the salmon fillets on top of the asparagus. Sprinkle with the sesame seeds. Set in your oven.
4.Cover and bake for 12 to 17 minutes, until the salmon flakes with a fork and the asparagus is tender.
5.Garnish the salmon with the chopped scallions before serving.

Nutritional value per serving: Calories: 321.3 kcal, Protein: 39.9g, Fat: 16.1g, Carbs: 1.8g

Italian Fisherman's Stew

Tomatoes, onions, and fennel flavor this light and healthy fish stew. This dish is good as a first course to start off a holiday dinner, or just perfect to make on a busy weeknight.

Preparation time and cooking time: 35 minutes | Serves: 4

Ingredients To Use:

- 2 tablespoons extra-virgin olive oil

- 1 medium onion, chopped

- 1 fennel bulb, chopped, a few fronds reserved for garnish

- 1 (14-ounce) can diced tomatoes with garlic and basil

- 1 cup low-sodium chicken or vegetable broth (store-bought or homemade)

- 1 teaspoon seasoned salt

- ½ teaspoon freshly ground black pepper

- 8 ounces white fish fillets (such as tilapia or cod), cut into 1- to 2-inch pieces

- 8 ounces shrimp, peeled and deveined, tails removed

Step-by-Step Directions to cook it:

1. Start heating the olive oil in the medium heated Lodge Cast Iron Dutch Oven. Add the onion and fennel and sauté for 10 minutes or until the vegetables are soft.
2. Add the tomatoes, broth, seasoned salt, and pepper, cover, and cook for 10 minutes over medium heat, stirring once or twice.
3. Gently stir in the fish and shrimp. Reduce the heat to low and simmer for 5 minutes, until the shrimp are no longer pink and the fish flakes with a fork. Garnish with the reserved fennel fronds before serving.

Nutritional value per serving: Calories: 436 kcal, Protein: 48g, Fat: 10g, Carbs: 24g

Low Country Shrimp Boil

I will often make this dinner for my family when we are on vacation. We rent a house at the Jersey Shore, and there is always super-fresh shrimp available.

Preparation time and cooking time: 30 minutes | Serves: 4

Ingredients To Use:

•1½ cups beer

•¼ cup Old Bay or Cajun seasoning

•1 pound small baby red potatoes

•4 ears of corn, husked and cut into thirds

•1 pound unpeeled large raw shrimp

OPTIONAL

•Cocktail sauce

•Lemon wedges

Step-by-Step Directions to cook it:

1.Prepae your oven.
2.Fill a pot halfway with water. Add the beer and seasoning. Cover and bring to a boil over medium-high heat, then reduce the heat to low so the liquid is simmering.
3.Add the potatoes and cook until just tender, about 10 minutes. Add the corn and cook for 5 more minutes.
4.Add the shrimp and cook for 3 to 5 minutes, until they turn pink and are fully cooked. Remove the pot from the heat and drain the cooking liquid from the pot.
5.This shrimp boil can be served right in the Lodge Cast Iron Dutch Oven. Serve with cocktail sauce and lemon wedges on the side, if desired.

Nutritional value per serving: Calories: 206.6 kcal, Protein: 20.5g, Fat: 5.1g, Carbs: 32.7g

Shrimp Stir-Fry with Honey-Garlic Sauce

This shrimp stir-fry is healthy, packed with flavor, and such an easy meal to make. Frozen vegetables help get dinner on the table in 30 minutes or less—quicker than waiting for delivery.

Preparation time and cooking time: 25 minutes | Serves: 4

Ingredients To Use:

- •3 tablespoons honey
- •3 tablespoons low-sodium soy sauce
- •3 garlic cloves, chopped
- •1 pound large shrimp, peeled and deveined, tails removed
- •2 tablespoons extra-virgin olive oil
- •1 pound frozen Asian stir-fry vegetables

OPTIONAL

- •2 scallions, white and green parts, chopped

Step-by-Step Directions to cook it:

1. In a medium bowl, whisk together the honey, soy sauce, and garlic. Add the shrimp and mix well. Set aside for 10 minutes.
2. When the shrimp have been marinating for about 6 minutes, Start heating the olive oil in the medium heated Lodge Cast Iron Dutch Oven. Add the vegetables and cook for about 4 minutes, until softened. Add the shrimp with the sauce, and cook for about 3 minutes or until the shrimp begin to turn pink. Continue to cook for 3 to 5 more minutes, until the shrimp and vegetables are well coated and the sauce starts to thicken.
3. Sprinkle with scallions before serving, if desired.

Nutritional value per serving: Calories: 376.7 kcal, Protein: 27g, Fat: 9.8g, Carbs: 49.4g

Roasted Red Pepper Crab Cakes

You don't have to go to Maryland for great crab cakes, as they're easy to make at home. I especially love the sweet roasted red peppers in this version. They have very little filler ingredients, with just enough panko bread crumbs to make them light and crispy.

Preparation time and cooking time: 60 minutes | Serves: 6

Ingredients To Use:

- 1 pound crab meat
- ⅓ cup mayonnaise
- 1 teaspoon seasoned salt, plus more to taste
- ½ cup panko bread crumbs

- 1 egg, beaten
- ½ cup roasted red bell peppers, finely chopped
- 2 to 3 tablespoons extra-virgin olive oil
- Freshly ground black pepper

Optional

- Buns
- Tartar sauce and/or cocktail sauce

Step-by-Step Directions to cook it:

1. In a medium bowl, mix together the crab meat, mayonnaise, seasoned salt, panko crumbs, egg, and roasted red peppers. Divide the mixture and use your hands to form 6 patties. Place the patties a plate, cover with plastic wrap, and chill in the refrigerator for 30 minutes.
2. Heat enough oil to coat the bottom of a pot set in the Lodge Cast Iron Dutch Oven over medium heat. Gently add the crab cakes to the pot, and cook for 5 to 6 minutes on each side, until the cakes are cooked through and golden brown. You may want to do this in batches, as all the crab cakes will probably not fit in the pot at once. Add another tablespoon of oil to the pot, if needed, for the second batch.
3. Season with seasoned salt and pepper before serving—on buns with sauce, if using.

Nutritional value per serving: Calories: 383 kcal, Protein: 15.1g, Fat: 33.8g, Carbs: 4.9g

Mussels with Italian-Spiced Tomato Broth

I grew up in northern New Jersey, where every pizza place also made great mussels in red sauce. We always had an order of mussels with our pizza on Friday nights.

Preparation time and cooking time: 40 minutes | Serves: 4

Ingredients To Use:

• 2 pounds fresh mussels, soaked and cleaned

• 2 tablespoons extra-virgin olive oil

• 1 tablespoon crushed garlic

• 1 (14-ounce) can diced fire-roasted tomatoes

• ½ cup white wine

• 1 cup vegetable broth

• 1 tablespoon Italian seasoning (store-bought or homemade)

• Salt

• Freshly ground black pepper

Step-by-Step Directions to cook it:

1. Make sure the mussels are well cleaned (see Tip).
2. In a pot set in the Lodge Cast Iron Dutch Oven over medium heat, heat the olive oil. Add the garlic, tomatoes, wine, broth, and Italian seasoning. Cover and bring the sauce to a simmer. This should take about 10 minutes. Reduce the heat to low and cook for 10 minutes more.
3. Add the mussels to the pot. Toss, then cover and cook for about 5 minutes, until the mussels open up. Make sure to discard any mussels that don't open during cooking.
4. Season with salt and pepper, and serve right from the pot.

Nutritional value per serving: Calories: 429.4 kcal, Protein: 27.1g, Fat: 20 g, Carbs: 76.3g

Fresh Clams with Butter Sauce and Spaghetti

My daughter was six years old when we took her to a restaurant for a Mother's Day dinner. It was her first time at a fancy restaurant, and I remember exactly what she ordered: linguine with white clam sauce.

Preparation time and cooking time: 60 minutes | Serves: 6

Ingredients To Use:

- 1 pound spaghetti
- 2 tablespoons extra-virgin olive oil
- 4 garlic cloves, chopped
- 1 cup vegetable or chicken broth (store-bought or homemade, here)

- 3 dozen little neck clams (about 3 to 4 pounds total), cleaned and prepared (see tip)
- 3 tablespoons butter
- ¼ cup chopped fresh parsley, plus more for garnish
- Salt
- Freshly ground black pepper

Step-by-Step Directions to cook it:

1. Fill a pot with water, set on your Lodge Cast Iron Dutch Oven and bring it to a boil over high heat. Add the pasta and cook for 8 to 10 minutes, until almost al dente. Reserve 1 cup of the pasta water, then drain the pasta and keep it warm.
2. Return the pot to the Lodge Cast Iron Dutch Oven over medium-high heat. Add the olive oil and garlic. Sauté for about 2 minutes, until the garlic starts to turn golden. Stir in the broth and add the clams.
3. Increase the heat to high. Give the clams a quick stir, cover the pot, and cook for 4 to 6 minutes, until the clams are steamed and have opened. Use a slotted spoon to transfer the cooked clams to a big bowl. Discard any clams that have broken shells or haven't opened.
4. Add the reserved pasta water to the pot, and bring it to a boil. Reduce the heat to low. Add the butter and parsley, stirring constantly until the butter is melted. Add the pasta, and toss well with the sauce. Cook for a few minutes, until the pasta is well coated and the sauce has thickened.
5. Remove the pot from the heat and transfer the pasta to individual bowls. Season with salt and pepper. Top with the clams and any juices that have accumulated on the plate. Garnish with extra parsley, if desired, before serving.

Nutritional value per serving: Calories: 276 kcal, Protein: 18g, Fat: 4.8g, Carbs: 44g

Chapter 4: Chicken & Poultry Recipes

Lodge Cast Iron Dutch Oven Chicken Cacciatore

You can find as many chicken cacciatore recipes as there are Italian grandparents who make them. For dipping, a chicken cacciatore worthy of its bread is rustic, richly flavored, and speaks to the part of us who wants warmth and familiarity.

Preparation time and cooking time: 40 minutes | Serves: 6-8

Ingredients To Use:

- 1 tablespoon olive oil
- 2 pounds chicken breasts and thighs, diced
- 1 teaspoon oregano
- 1 teaspoon basil
- ½ teaspoon salt
- ½ teaspoon black pepper
- 1 small onion, diced

- 1 red bell pepper (thin strips)
- 1 yellow bell pepper cut into thin strips
- 1 cup sliced mushrooms
- 3 cloves garlic, minced
- 1 (20-ounce) can crushed tomatoes
- 2 cups low-Sodium chicken broth
- 2 ½ cups small dry pasta (like penne)

Step-by-Step Directions to cook it:

1. Place your pot in the Lodge Cast Iron Dutch Oven set to medium heat (a 12-inch pot would go over 18 briquettes) and warm the oil. Add the chicken and brown it on all sides. Season it with oregano, basil, salt, and pepper.
2. Add the vegetables and stir. Cook until they begin to soften, often stirring, about 3 minutes.
3. Add the crushed tomatoes, chicken broth, and pasta.
4. Bring the pot to a boil and cover it with the lid. Adjust its position on the coals to keep it simmering for about 20 minutes or until the pasta is cooked, stirring once or twice. Keep the lid off for the last few minutes if the sauce is too runny.

Nutritional value per serving: Calories: 430 kcal, Protein: 40.5g, Fat: 8.4g, Carbs: 46g

Chicken Vegetable Pasta Bake

This Pasta Bake for Chicken and Vegetables is a simple concept for dinner made with chicken, vegetables and pasta. A sweet homemade pasta with lovely colors and an outstanding taste!

Preparation time and cooking time: 60 minutes | Serves: 4

Ingredients To Use:

- 1 small onion, thinly sliced
- 1 (28 oz.) can tomatoes
- 1 teaspoon basil
- 1 teaspoon oregano
- 2 cups shell pasta
- 1 1/2 lbs chicken thighs

- 1/2 teaspoon salt
- 1/4 teaspoon of pepper
- 5 garlic cloves, crushed
- 1 cup carrots, sliced
- 1 cup eggplant, thinly sliced
- ½ cup corn kernels
- 1 green apple, sliced

Step-by-Step Directions to cook it:

1. Preheat your Lodge Cast Iron Dutch Oven.
2. Coat the base and sides of a pot with non- stick cooking spray.
3. Spread the onions evenly over the base of the pan.
4. Drain the tomatoes, reserving the juice and setting the tomatoes aside.
5. Add enough water to the tomato juice to make one cup of liquid.
6. Add basil, oregano and marjoram to the juice and stir until well blended.
7. Place the pasta into the pan, making an even layer over the onions. Pour 3/4 cup the tomato juice mixture over the pasta.
8. Place the chicken in an even layer over the pasta and season with salt and pepper. Sprinkle garlic over the chicken.
9. Spread the tomatoes in one even layer over the chicken then add vegetables and apple.
10. Pour the remaining tomato juice mixture over the ingredients.
11. Cover and bake 45 minutes or until the chicken is cooked through.

Nutritional value per serving: Calories: 379.2 kcal, Protein: 26g, Fat: 11.6g, Carbs: 39.7g

Chicken Meatballs and Pasta

Chicken Meatballs-these are Fried, tiny golden balls that are juicy on the inside, bursting with savory flavor, so they keep their pleasant round shape and, honestly, it's just much easier than frying the pan!

Preparation time and cooking time: 65 minutes | Serves: 4

Ingredients To Use:

- 3 cups small pasta
- 1 teaspoon olive oil
- 2/3 cup of water
- 1 lb. ground chicken
- 1 egg, lightly beaten
- 1/2 cup of bread crumbs
- Salt and pepper
- 2 (12 oz.) jars of marinara sauce, divided
- 3 carrots, sliced into coins
- 1 small zucchini, halved lengthwise and cut into slices
- 1 yellow bell pepper, cored, seeded and cut into strips

Step-by-Step Directions to cook it:

1. Preheat your oven.
2. Place the chicken into a mixing bowl.
3. Add the egg, breadcrumbs, salt and pepper and mix until well blended.
4. Shape the mixture into meatballs.
5. Spray a cooking pan with a non-stick cooking spray, so base, sides and lid are well coated.
6. Place the pasta into the pan and drizzle with olive oil.
7. Pour in the water, stirring to coat the pasta well, then pour one jar of marinara sauce over the pasta.
8. Add layers of carrots, zucchini, and bell pepper strips and pour the second jar of sauce over the vegetables.
9. Cover and bake 45 minutes or until the vegetables are fork tender.

Nutritional value per serving: Calories: 239 kcal, Protein: 27g, Fat: 14g, Carbs: 0g

One Pot Chicken Rigatoni

All the fantastic flavors of chicken parmesan, blended in one simple one-pot pasta dish, ready in 30 minutes! Few dishes, but a maximum-flavored meal!

Preparation time and cooking time: 25 minutes | Serves: 4

Ingredients To Use:

- 2 tablespoons extra virgin olive oil
- 1-pound chicken breast, diced
- 2 red peppers, sliced into thin strips
- 1 (28-ounce) can crushed tomatoes
- 2 cups chicken broth
- 1-pound dry rigatoni
- 2 teaspoons Italian seasoning
- ½ cup Parmesan cheese
- ¼ cup butter
- ¼ cup heavy cream
- Crushed red pepper flakes, optional

Step-by-Step Directions to cook it:

1. Place a pot over medium heat (about 20 briquettes) and warm the oil.
2. Brown the chicken breast.
3. Add the red pepper strips and sauté for about two minutes, until they begin to soften.
4. Add the crushed tomatoes, chicken broth, rigatoni, and Italian seasoning.
5. Cover the pot, and place 6 briquettes on top.
6. Bring it to a boil and cook for 10–15 minutes, until the pasta is ready.
7. Remove the pot from the heat and stir in the Parmesan, butter, and cream.
8. Cover, and let it sit for 5 minutes.
9. Serve garnished with additional Parmesan and crushed red pepper flakes to taste.

Nutritional value per serving: Calories: 613.5 kcal, Protein: 38.2g, Fat: 7.8g, Carbs: 70.8g

Chicken and Squash One-Pot Meal

This One Pan Chicken and Squash Meal, with roasted butternut squash, is a simple baked chicken recipe.

Preparation time and cooking time: 2 hours | Serves: 4

- 1 (3–4 pound) fryer/boiler chicken
- 2 teaspoons salt
- 4 cups 1-inch dry bread cubes
- 2 cups butternut squash, cut into ½-inch cubes
- ½ large red onion, chopped
- 4 sprigs fresh thyme

Step-by-Step Directions to cook it:

1. Preheat the oven to 375°F (190°C). Place a rack in the lower third.
2. Pat the chicken dry and season evenly with salt.
3. Layer the bread cubes and squash over the bottom of the Lodge Cast Iron Dutch Oven. Add the thyme on top.
4. Make a well in the center of the Lodge Cast Iron Dutch Oven and place the chicken in the well. Insert a cooking thermometer in its thigh.
5. Cover and bake for 1 hour.
6. Remove the lid and continue to bake for 30 more minutes until the chicken is golden, tender, and crisp. The juices should run clear and the cooking thermometer should read 165°F.
7. Let cool for a while and then shred the meat.
8. Serve with the cooked squash and bread mixture.

Nutritional value per serving: Calories: 992 kcal, Protein: 79g, Fat: 61g, Carbs: 27g

Cheesy Baked Chicken Spaghetti Casserole

THE BEST! Chicken, spaghetti, chicken soup sauce, sour cream, butter, seasonings, Parmesan and cheddar cheese Once a month, we build this! Make a delicious freezer meal!

Preparation time and cooking time: 65 minutes | Serves: 8

Ingredients To Use:

- 4 bone-in chicken thighs with skin
- 1 teaspoon Italian seasoning
- Salt and pepper to taste
- 1 dash balsamic vinegar

- 1 pound Italian sausages
- ½ pound mushrooms, sliced
- 3 cups spaghetti sauce
- 1 pound spaghetti
- 2 cups shredded Italian cheese blend

Step-by-Step Directions to cook it:

1. Preheat the Lodge Cast Iron Dutch Oven to 350°F (175°C).
2. Boil salted water in a pot and cook the spaghetti partially for 4 minutes. Drain and set aside.
3. Spray the pot with cooking spray and heat it over medium-high heat.
4. Add the chicken thighs and stir-cook for 3 minutes per side until evenly browned.
5. Season with salt, Italian seasoning, and pepper. Transfer to a plate and sprinkle vinegar on top.
6. Add the sausage and mushrooms to the pot; stir-cook for 4–5 minutes until evenly browned. Drain and remove residual grease.
7. Add the spaghetti sauce and cooked chicken (skin side up).
8. Cook for 3–5 minutes until the sauce is bubbly.
9. Cover and bake for 30 minutes.
10. Add the spaghetti noodles and Italian cheese blend on top; bake for 10 more minutes until cooked to satisfaction.
11. Serve warm.

Nutritional value per serving: Calories: 614 kcal, Protein: 33g, Fat: 27g, Carbs: 58g

Chicken Stew a la Bonne Femme

This recipe can be made with 3 pounds of bone-in chicken breast halves or pieces of your choice.

Preparation time and cooking time: 3 hours & 15 minutes | Serves: 4-6

Ingredients To Use:

- 1 pound bacon
- 1 (3-pound) chicken, cut into pieces
- 3 pounds white potatoes, peeled and cut in chunks
- 2 large onions, peeled and chopped
- 1 large green bell pepper, seeded and chopped
- 2 stalks celery, sliced
- 3 cloves garlic, peeled and minced
- 2 green onions, sliced
- 1/4 cup minced parsley
- 1/2 teaspoon salt
- 1/2 teaspoon freshly cracked black pepper
- 1/4 teaspoon cayenne pepper
- 3 cups chicken broth

Step-by-Step Directions to cook it:

1. In an ovenproof pot over medium heat fry bacon until crisp and the fat has rendered, about 8–10 minutes. Remove bacon to a paper towel–lined plate to drain.
2. Add chicken to bacon drippings remaining in pot and brown well on both sides, about 3 minutes per side. Remove to a plate to rest. Add potato chunks to pot; brown on all sides, about 5 minutes, and remove to rest with the chicken.
3. In a medium bowl, combine onions, bell pepper, celery, garlic, green onions, and parsley; mix well. In a small bowl combine salt, pepper, and cayenne.
4. Heat oven to 350°F.
5. Carefully remove all but 1 or 2 tablespoons of the bacon drippings from pot. Layer the ingredients in Lodge Cast Iron Dutch Oven in following order: 1/2 each of chicken, potatoes, bacon, vegetable mixture, and seasonings; remaining potatoes, bacon, chicken, vegetable mixture, and seasonings.
6. Carefully pour broth into the Lodge Cast Iron Dutch Oven, cover with the lid, and roast for 2 1/2 hours. Let stand 10 minutes before serving.

Nutritional value per serving: Calories: 1097.87 kcal, Protein: 75.56g, Fat: 51.18g, Carbs: 78.9g

Chicken Fricassee

Chicken fricassee tops many folks' comfort food lists. This version smells heavenly while cooking. Serve this dish over rice.

Preparation time and cooking time: 1 hour & 55 minutes | Serves: 4

Ingredients To Use:

- 1 teaspoon salt
- 1/2 teaspoon freshly ground black pepper
- 1/2 teaspoon cayenne pepper
- 1/2 teaspoon garlic powder
- 1 (4-pound) chicken, cut into 8 pieces
- 1/2 cup vegetable oil
- 2/3 cup all-purpose flour
- 1 large onion, peeled and diced, divided
- 6 cups chicken broth
- 1 large green bell pepper, seeded and diced
- Pinch thyme
- 3 green onions, minced

Step-by-Step Directions to cook it:

1. Combine salt, pepper, cayenne, and garlic powder in a small bowl. Sprinkle the seasonings over the chicken.
2. Heat a pot over medium-high heat. Add oil and once it shimmers add chicken and brown well on both sides, about 5 minutes per side. Remove chicken to a plate to rest.
3. Add flour into hot oil and cook, stirring constantly, until flour turns dark brown, about 8–10 minutes. Add 1/2 of onion and cook until fragrant, about 1 minute.
4. Carefully add the broth, stirring constantly, until flour mixture is dissolved in broth. Return chicken to pot along with remaining onion, bell pepper, and thyme.
5. Reduce heat to medium and cook, stirring occasionally, for 11/2 hours, or until chicken is tender and sauce is thick. Stir in green onions.

Nutritional value per serving: Calories: 219.5 kcal, Protein: 27.8g, Fat: 6.6g, Carbs: 9.2 g

Chicken Divan

This is a versatile casserole. You can stretch it to 8 servings by adding 1–2 cups of cooked diced potatoes. You can also substitute American, Cheddar, or Swiss cheese for the Parmigiano-Reggiano.

Preparation time and cooking time: 55 minutes | Serves: 6

Ingredients To Use:

- 1/4 cup unsalted butter
- 1/4 cup all-purpose flour
- 1 cup chicken broth
- 1 cup milk
- 1/2 teaspoon salt
- 1/2 teaspoon freshly cracked black pepper
- 1/8 teaspoon ground nutmeg
- 1/2 cup freshly grated Parmigiano-Reggiano, divided
- 3 tablespoons dry sherry
- 3 cups cooked chicken, cut into bite-sized pieces
- 1 (1-pound) bag broccoli florets, thawed
- 1 cup slivered almonds, divided
- 1/2 cup heavy cream

Step-by-Step Directions to cook it:

1. Heat oven to 350°F.
2. Melt butter over medium heat in a cooking pan. Add flour and cook, stirring constantly, 1 minute.
3. Gradually whisk in broth and milk; cook 3 minutes, or until it begins to thicken. Stir in salt, pepper, nutmeg, 1/4 cup cheese, and sherry; cook until cheese melts.
4. Remove from heat and stir in the chicken, broccoli, half of almonds, and cream. Sprinkle remaining almonds and cheese over the top. Bake uncovered 35 minutes, or until bubbly and golden brown.

Nutritional value per serving: Calories: 242.9 kcal, Protein: 22.4g, Fat: 10.1g, Carbs: 15g

Golden Fried Chicken Tenders

Chicken tenders are easier and faster to prepare than bone-in fried chicken, and can be an appetizer with dipping sauces for a party, a main dish with mashed potatoes for dinner, or added to green salads for a speedy lunch!

Preparation time and cooking time: 30 minutes | Serves: 4-6

Ingredients To Use:

- 1 cup all-purpose flour
- 1 teaspoon salt
- 1 teaspoon freshly cracked black pepper
- 2 large eggs, beaten
- 1 cup buttermilk
- 1 teaspoon hot sauce, optional
- 2 pounds chicken tenders
- Oil, for frying

Step-by-Step Directions to cook it:

1. In a large zip-top bag add flour, salt, and pepper. Shake well to coat.
2. In a shallow dish or pie pan add eggs and buttermilk. Whisk to combine, then add hot sauce, if desired, and whisk to incorporate.
3. Add a few tenders at a time to flour, toss to coat, then remove from the bag, shaking off any excess flour. Dip tenders into buttermilk mixture, allowing any excess to drip off, then return tenders to flour and toss again to coat. Transfer coated tenders to a wire rack to dry while you prepare remaining tenders.
4. In a cooking pot, heat 3" oil over medium-high heat to 350°F, making sure there is a 3" air gap at the top of the pot. Once oil is hot add 3–4 tenders at a time and fry until golden brown and floating, about 3 minutes per side. Transfer to a clean wire rack over a sheet pan to drain. You may store cooked tenders in a warm oven while you fry the rest.

Nutritional value per serving: Calories: 87 kcal, Protein: 7.2g, Fat: 4.1g, Carbs: 5.5g

Whole Roast Chicken with Fresh Herbs

This chicken makes an impressive Sunday supper, and leftovers can be chopped up for chicken salad, or shredded and added to soups and stews, such as Old-Fashioned Chicken and Dumplings.

Preparation time and cooking time: 1 hour and 30 minutes | Serves: 4-6

Ingredients To Use:

- 1 (2–3 pound) whole chicken
- 2 teaspoons kosher salt
- 1 teaspoon freshly cracked black pepper
- 1 small bundle fresh thyme
- 1 small bundle fresh sage
- 2 sprigs fresh rosemary
- 1 medium lemon, cut into 4 wedges

Step-by-Step Directions to cook it:

1. Heat oven to 450°F. Place an ovenproof skillet into oven to heat.
2. Pat chicken dry inside and out with paper towels, then coat the outside of chicken with salt and pepper, making sure to rub the spices into the skin evenly.
3. Stuff the cavity of the bird with fresh herbs and lemon wedges. Truss the bird by tying the legs together with butcher's twine, then wrapping twine around the base of the bird so the wings are held close to the body.
4. Carefully transfer chicken to the heated Lodge Cast Iron Dutch Oven. Roast 50–60 minutes or until the juices from the thigh run clear and the internal temperature of the breast and thigh reach 160°F.
5. Allow chicken to rest 15 minutes. Remove and discard the twine and herbs and lemon from the chicken cavity and serve.

Nutritional value per serving: Calories: 370 kcal, Protein: 47g, Fat: 9g, Carbs: 25g

Buttermilk Roasted Chicken Legs

These chicken legs are tender, moist, and very juicy. They can be served hot or cold, so you can make these the night before for a picnic or potluck meal where you need a cold dish.

Preparation time and cooking time: 12 hours | Serves: 4

Ingredients To Use:

•2 cups buttermilk

•1 tablespoon maple syrup

•1 teaspoon smoked paprika

•1/2 teaspoon salt

•1/2 teaspoon freshly cracked black pepper

•1/2 teaspoon poultry seasoning

•1/2 teaspoon hot sauce

•8 chicken drumsticks, about 11/2 pounds

Step-by-Step Directions to cook it:

1.In a large zip-top bag add all of ingredients except chicken. Close the bag and shake to combine then add chicken, seal the bag, and refrigerate 4 hours or overnight.
2.Remove chicken from the buttermilk and place in a colander 30 minutes to drain.
3.Heat oven to 400°F. Place an ovenproof cooking pan into oven to heat.
4.Once heated, lightly spray the pan with nonstick cooking spray. Arrange drumsticks in the bottom of the pan in a single layer. Roast 35–45 minutes, turning the legs halfway through, or until chicken legs reach an internal temperature of 160°F and the juices run clear.

Nutritional value per serving: Calories: 531 kcal, Protein: 46g, Fat: 34g, Carbs: 7g

Coq Au Vin

This classic French dish, like so many others, was created to get the most out of the ingredients a farm kitchen was likely to have on hand.

Preparation time and cooking time: 2 hours and 30 minutes | Serves: 4-5

Ingredients To Use:

- 4 slices bacon
- 1 cup plus 2 tablespoons all-purpose flour, divided
- 1 teaspoon salt
- 1/4 teaspoon ground pepper
- 1 fryer chicken cut into 8 pieces, or 3–4 pounds of chicken thighs
- 1 cup chicken broth

- 2 cups dry red wine
- 2 tablespoons Dijon mustard
- 2 cloves garlic, peeled and minced
- 3–4 sprigs fresh thyme
- 3 bay leaves
- 2 medium celery stalks, diced
- 2 large carrots, diced
- 1 medium onion, peeled and diced

Step-by-Step Directions to cook it:

1. Heat oven to 325°F.
2. Place an ovenproof pan over medium heat. Cut bacon strip and put it to the pot. Fry until crispiness, then remove and reserve for another use. Drain all but 1 tablespoon of the drippings.
3. Combine 1 cup flour, salt, and pepper in a wide, shallow bowl. Dredge chicken pieces through flour and place them skin side down in the pan. Cook 3–4 minutes on each side, or until they're lightly honey-colored. Cook in batches if necessary.
4. Remove chicken once it's cooked. Add broth, wine, mustard, and garlic to pot, turn off heat, and place chicken back in the pan. Among the chicken bits are Tuck Thyme and Bay Leaves. Sprinkle the chicken with the celery, carrots, and onion on top. Cover it and place it in the oven. 2-21/2 hours of cooking.
5. Remove chicken and vegetables to a large bowl and cover to keep warm. Discard thyme and bay leaves. Place the pan over medium-high heat and let most of the liquid evaporate. Whisk in the remaining 2 tablespoons reserved flour quickly to keep from getting lumps. Once you have thick gravy, about 3 minutes, pour it over chicken pieces in bowl and serve warm.

Nutritional value per serving: Calories: 272 kcal, Protein: 30g, Fat: 11g, Carbs: 13g

Chapter 5: Vegan & Vegetarian Recipes

Easy Minestrone Soup

Minestrone is a hearty Italian vegetable soup with a tomato base. Frozen vegetables make this soup easy to cook any time you want it. Often, if I am in a dinner-ingredient dilemma, minestrone is an easy winner.

Preparation time and cooking time: 45 minutes | Serves: 4

Ingredients To Use:

- 1 tablespoon extra-virgin olive oil
- 1 small yellow onion, chopped
- 1 (14-ounce) can diced fire-roasted tomatoes
- 8 cups vegetable broth
- 2 cups uncooked small elbow pasta
- 1 pound frozen soup vegetables
- 1 (15-ounce) can red kidney beans, drained and rinsed
- Salt
- Freshly ground black pepper

Step-by-Step Directions to cook it:

1. Set Lodge Cast Iron Dutch Oven over medium-high heat, add the olive oil in a pan and heat. Put the onion and sauté for 5 minutes or until translucent. Put the tomatoes and vegetable broth and cook over medium heat for 5 to 10 minutes, until the liquid comes to a boil.
2. Add the pasta, soup vegetables, and beans. Bring to a boil, reduce the heat to low, cover, and simmer for 20 to 25 minutes, until the pasta is tender. Season with salt and pepper before serving.

Nutritional value per serving: Calories: 315 kcal, Protein: 15g, Fat: 10g, Carbs: 43g

Veggie Fried Rice

Fried rice is the dish I make when I have leftovers that need repurposing. This basic vegetarian fried rice comes out best when you use rice that has been chilled in the refrigerator.

Preparation time and cooking time: 40 minutes | Serves: 4

Ingredients To Use:

- •3 tablespoons butter, divided
- •1 (10-ounce) package frozen peas and carrots
- •3 cups leftover cooked rice, cold
- •3 tablespoons low-sodium soy sauce (gluten-free if needed), plus more for serving
- •2 eggs, beaten
- •Freshly ground black pepper

Step-by-Step Directions to cook it:

6. Set a pot in a Lodge Cast Iron Dutch Oven preheated medium-high heat, heat 1 tablespoon of the butter. Add the frozen peas and carrots. Sauté for about 5 minutes, until the peas and carrots are soft.

7. Increase the heat to high, add the remaining 2 tablespoons of butter, and stir until melted. Immediately add the rice and soy sauce, and stir until combined. Continue cooking, stirring constantly, for 3 more minutes to fry the rice.

8. Push the fried rice to one side of the pot, and add the eggs to the other side. Stir well so the eggs are scrambled while cooking. Mix the cooked eggs into the rice.

9. Remove from the heat. Season with pepper and more soy sauce before serving.

Nutritional value per serving: Calories: 202 kcal, Protein: 3.2g, Fat: 9g, Carbs: 27.3g

Spring Vegetable Risotto with Parmesan

When I make this creamy risotto dish, I am instantly transported back to my Nana's house. She would serve this in a huge bowl, family style, for my aunts, uncles, and cousins.

Preparation time and cooking time: 70 minutes | Serves: 4

Ingredients To Use:

- •5 cups chicken broth (store-bought or homemade, here), divided, plus more if needed
- •1 cup frozen peas
- •½ pound asparagus, trimmed and cut into bite-size pieces
- •1½ cups arborio rice
- •1 cup freshly grated Parmesan cheese
- •3 tablespoons salted butter, cut into pieces
- •Salt
- •Freshly ground black pepper

Step-by-Step Directions to cook it:

1. Preheat the Lodge Cast Iron Dutch Oven to 350°F.
2. Pour 4 cups of the chicken broth into a pot. Turn the heat to medium-high and cook until the broth comes to a boil, 5 to 10 minutes. Stir in the peas, asparagus, and rice, and mix well.
3. Cover the pot, transfer it to the oven, and bake for 40 minutes or until most of the liquid is absorbed and the rice is tender.
4. Remove the risotto from the oven. Microwave the remaining cup of chicken broth for 2 minutes. Stir the heated broth, Parmesan cheese, and butter into the pot. Continue to stir vigorously for 2 to 3 minutes, until the rice is very creamy. (You can add extra warm broth to thin the risotto if necessary.) Season with salt and pepper before serving.

Nutritional value per serving: Calories: 347 kcal, Protein: 11g, Fat: 9g, Carbs: 50g

Penne with Chickpeas and Greens

My dad always referred to chickpeas as cici beans, because that's what they are called in Italian. My daughter makes this dish often at college.

Preparation time and cooking time: 40 minutes | Serves: 4

Ingredients To Use:

- 1 (16-ounce) box penne pasta
- 2 tablespoons extra-virgin olive oil
- 1 (15-ounce) can chickpeas, drained and rinsed
- 10 to 12 ounces baby greens, such as spinach
- 2 cups marinara sauce (store-bought or homemade, here)
- ⅓ cup grated Parmesan cheese, plus more for serving
- Salt
- Freshly ground black pepper

Step-by-Step Directions to cook it:

1. Prepare your Lodge Cast Iron Dutch Oven.
2. Pour water in a large pot, and bring to a boil. Put the pasta and cook for 10 to 12 minutes (or per package directions), until al dente. Drain in a colander, reserving ½ cup of pasta water, and keep warm.
3. In the pot, heat the olive oil. Place the chickpeas and greens. Cook for about 5 minutes or until the greens are wilted.
4. Put the cooked pasta, marinara sauce, and reserved pasta water. Reduce the heat to low and cook for another 5 to 10 minutes, until the sauce is thickened and bubbly.
5. Transfer the pasta mixture to a large bowl, and mix in the Parmesan cheese. Season with salt and pepper. Serve with extra Parmesan cheese on top.

Nutritional value per serving: Calories: 220 kcal, Protein: 13g, Fat: 3.5g, Carbs: 33g

Lodge Cast Iron Dutch Oven Smoked Gouda Mac and Cheese

Every home cook should have a good macaroni and cheese recipe. I like making mine on the stove so I can skip heating up the oven on a hot day.

Preparation time and cooking time: 35 minutes | Serves: 6

Ingredients To Use:

- 1 (16-ounce) box medium pasta shells
- 3 tablespoons butter
- ⅓ cup all-purpose flour
- 4 cups low-fat milk
- 1 teaspoon salt
- 8 ounces mild cheddar cheese, shredded
- 8 ounces smoked Gouda cheese, shredded

Step-by-Sstep Directions to cook it:

1. Prepare your Lodge Cast Iron Dutch Oven.
2. Fill a pot with water, and bring to a boil. Add the pasta shells and cook according to package instructions for al dente (about 6 to 8 minutes). Drain well and keep warm.
3. Add the butter to the pot, and melt it. Stir in the flour, and keep stirring to form a thick paste. Mix with a wire whisk, and slowly add the milk and salt. Cook over medium heat for about 10 minutes, until the sauce is thickened and simmering. Make sure to constantly stir to remove any lumps in the sauce.
4. Add both cheeses, a handful at a time, and mix well until the sauce is smooth and thick.
5. Stir in the cooked pasta, and combine well until the pasta is well coated with the cheese sauce. Cook for another 5 minutes, until the pasta is heated through and the sauce has thickened. Serve warm in bowls.

Nutritional value per serving: Calories: 710 kcal, Protein: 37g, Fat: 30g, Carbs: 73g

Deep-Dish Pizza in a Lodge Cast Iron Dutch Oven

I grew up on thin-crust New York–style pizza, but I also love deep dish–style from Chicago. After a visit there several years ago, I thought I'd try making some at home. The Lodge Cast Iron Dutch Oven is a perfect device for making deep-dish pizza.

Preparation time and cooking time: 65 minutes | Serves: 4

Ingredients To Use:

- 1 pound pizza dough, (store-bought or homemade), divided
- 1 tablespoon extra-virgin olive oil
- 1 cup marinara sauce (store-bought or homemade), divided
- 2 cups shredded mozzarella cheese, divided

Step-by-Step Directions to cook it:

1. Preheat the oven to 450°F. Place your pot (uncovered) on the lowest rack in your oven so it also preheats.
2. Roll half the pizza dough out to a 10- to 12-inch disk (about the size of the bottom of your Lodge Cast Iron Dutch Oven). Transfer the dough to a piece of parchment paper, and let it rest for about 10 minutes. If it starts to shrink, roll it out a bit more.
3. When the dough is ready, brush it with the olive oil, then spread ½ cup of the sauce on top of the dough. Top with 1 cup of the cheese. Slide the pizza, paper and all, onto a cutting board or pizza paddle to bring it to the oven. Carefully place the pizza in the Lodge Cast Iron Dutch Oven by holding onto the edges of the parchment paper and gently dropping it into the pot. The parchment paper will still be under the pizza.
4. Bake for about 15 to 20 minutes, until the crust is golden brown and the cheese is melted. Remove the pot from the oven, and use the parchment paper to lift the pizza out and onto a board. Cool for 5 minutes before slicing.
5. While you're eating the first pizza, repeat everything for the second pizza.

Nutritional value per serving: Calories: 350 kcal, Protein: 12g, Fat: 18g, Carbs: 34g

Green Beans with Butter and Shallots

The traditional French method of preparing the humble green bean is the tastiest by far. It is also very easy to make. Good, fresh salted butter is what gives it the sheen and flavor that will have guests asking for seconds, and thirds.

Preparation time and cooking time: 25 minutes | Serves: 4-6

Ingredients To Use:

•4 tablespoons butter, salted

•2 lbs. fresh French green beans

•4 shallots, chopped

•1 tablespoon salt

Step-by-Step Directions to cook it:

1.Prepare your oven.
2.Boil water, add salt, and plunge in the green beans, parboiling them for 4 minutes. Drain and put aside.
3.Heat butter for 30 seconds on medium heat, add shallots and stir.
4.Throw in green beans, and sauté, covered, mixing often, until just tender (about 10 minutes).
5.Let sit a few minutes covered before serving.
6.Add pepper as desired.

Nutritional value per serving: Calories: 70 kcal, Protein: 2g, Fat: 4g, Carbs: 6g

Sautéed Potatoes with Garlic and Parsley

Sautéed potatoes might seem like a simple dish, but it pairs so nicely with almost any main course that it is a real winner. Plus, a cast iron pot or skillet is perfect for getting just the right golden color.

Preparation time and cooking time: 40 minutes | Serves: 4-6

Ingredients To Use:

- •3 tablespoons olive oil
- •3 tablespoons butter
- •4 to 6 potatoes, cubed
- •2 cloves garlic, minced
- •1/2 cup minced parsley
- •Salt, to taste
- •Pepper, to taste

Step-by-Step Directions to cook it:

1. Prepare your oven.
2. Heat oil and butter for 30 seconds on medium heat, then add potatoes, roughly cut into cubes. Leaving the skin on is fine if potatoes are organic.
3. Sauté on medium heat, covering and stirring often, until golden on all sides and tender (about 20 to 30 minutes).
4. Add garlic, mix, and sauté an additional 5 minutes.
5. Add parsley, salt and pepper, mix, and serve hot.

Nutritional value per serving: Calories: 274 kcal, Protein: 5g, Fat: 17g, Carbs: 26g

Baked Stuffed Tomatoes

This is a great dish if you have leftover meat and/or rice. It cooks rapidly and is a tasty and succulent side dish or main course, depending on the stuffing used.

Preparation time and cooking time: 40 minutes | Serves: 4-6

Ingredients To Use:

- •2 tablespoons olive oil
- •4 cloves minced garlic
- •1 onion, minced
- •6 to 8 large tomatoes
- •1 cup cooked rice

- •2 cups cooked vegetable and/or meat, minced
- •1 tablespoon Herbes de Provence
- •1/2 cup parsley, minced
- •1 teaspoon salt
- •4 tablespoons bread crumbs
- •Additional olive oil

Step-by-Step Directions to cook it:

1. Prepare your Lodge Cast Iron Dutch Oven.
2. Cut one end off the tomatoes, and empty flesh. Put aside.
3. Heat oil for 30 seconds on medium heat, then add garlic and onion and stir. Cover and continue to cook on medium heat for 5-6 minutes, until beginning to get translucent. Stir every two minutes to prevent burning.
4. Remove and mix into pre-cooked rice, meat and/or vegetable, herbs, parsley and salt.
5. Add a little of the tomato flesh back into mixture, until blend is moist.
6. Stuff the tomatoes with mixture, packing it tightly.
7. Add a little oil to bottom of pot, and place stuffed tomatoes at bottom, packed tightly but not overlapping.
8. Cover with bread crumbs and a dash of olive oil.
9. Bake in oven at 350°F for 20 minutes.
10. Serve with sour cream.

Nutritional value per serving: Calories: 145 kcal, Protein: 24g, Fat: 45g, Carbs: 76g

A Basic Risotto

A very versatile grain is rice; and risotto (a way of cooking rice) is infinitely variable in terms of how it can be flavored and what can be added. From meat to shrimp to vegetables, a risotto can absorb many ingredients and flavors. A true dish to experiment with! Below is a good, basic risotto recipe. Think of it as your canvas.

Preparation time and cooking time: 35 minutes | Serves: 4-6

Ingredients To Use:

•2 tablespoons olive oil

•2 tablespoons butter, salted

•1 onion, chopped

•2 cups risotto rice, uncooked

•4 cups broth of choice

•1 cup parmesan, grated

Step-by-Step Directions to cook it:

1. Set your Lodge Cast Iron Dutch Oven ready.
2. Heat oil and butter for 30 seconds on medium heat, then add onion and stir.
3. Add rice, sauté, stirring.
4. Cover and continue to cook on medium heat for 5-6 minutes, until onion beginning to get translucent and rice opaque. Stir every two minutes to prevent burning.
5. Add broth, and cook about 13 to 15 minutes.
6. Add additional ingredients, if any, and cook about 5 more minutes. Optional additions (choose one): 2 tablespoons tomato paste; 1 cup finely chopped vegetable; 1 cup small, shelled shrimp; 1 cup chopped sausage.
7. Since cooking time will vary, when broth is absorbed and rice tender, the risotto is done.
8. Stir in grated parmesan just before serving.

Nutritional value per serving: Calories: 166 kcal, Protein: 5.2g, Fat: 7g, Carbs: 20g

Dreamy Baked Winter Vegetables with Feta

The creaminess of baked vegetables with feta cheese, tossed with a warm vinaigrette, is absolutely dreamy! A satisfying side dish for any meal.

Preparation time and cooking time: 50 minutes | Serves: 4-6

Ingredients To Use:

- ½ cup of cheese preferably shredded
- ¼ tsp of Italian seasoning

Taco seasoning

- 2 tablespoons olive oil
- 2 cloves garlic, chopped fine
- 1 onion, chopped fine
- 1 head of kale, chopped
- 2 cups of cubed squash (kombucha or other winter squash)

Vinaigrette

- 2 tablespoons olive oil
- 1 tablespoon balsamic vinegar

- 1 lb ground beef
- 1 egg

- 2 carrots, grated
- 1/2 cup walnuts, chopped and toasted
- 1/2 cup feta cheese, crumbled
- Salt, to taste
- Pepper, to taste
- Chopped parsley, for garnish

- 1 tablespoon Dijon mustard
- 1 minced shallot
- Salt to taste.

Step-by-Step Directions to cook it:

1. Preheat your Lodge Cast Iron Dutch Oven.
2. Put squash and kale in pot with 2 inches of boiling water. Cover and steam until soft, about 10 minutes.
3. Add grated carrot, stir, cover and cook for an additional 10 minutes.
4. Remove from heat when vegetables are tender.
5. Mix together vinaigrette ingredients. Warm in microwave, 10 seconds.
6. Pour warm vinaigrette over vegetables and mix well, then add walnuts, crumbled feta on top.
7. Salt and pepper to taste.. Serve immediately.

Nutritional value per serving: Calories: 319 kcal, Protein: 15g, Fat: 13g, Carbs: 36g

Tricolor Zucchini Bake

In the fall when there is an abundance of tomatoes and zucchini, one of my favorite dishes is made by baking these miracle vegetables with parmesan and olive oil. The flavor is so delicate and melts in the mouth. Great as a side dish for anything

Preparation time and cooking time: 60 minutes | Serves: 4

Ingredients To Use:

- •4 tablespoons olive oil
- •4 cloves garlic, minced fine
- •4 zucchinis, sliced into thin rounds
- •8 small tomatoes, sliced into rounds
- •1/2 cup parmesan cheese
- •2 tablespoons dried Herbs de Provence
- •Salt, to taste
- •Pepper, to taste
- •Chopped parsley, for garnish

Step-by-Step Directions to cook it:

1. Preheat your Lodge Cast Iron Dutch Oven.
2. Put 1 tablespoon olive oil into bottom of a cooking pan and spread evenly.
3. Place zucchini and tomato slices in distinct rows at the bottom of the pan. They should be stacked diagonally, in one layer only.
4. Drizzle with remaining olive oil, sprinkle with minced garlic, salt and herbs, and cover with Parmesan cheese.
5. Cover pot and bake in oven for 30 to 40 minutes at 350°F.
6. Remove from oven and let sit 10 minutes, covered, after checking that the vegetables are soft and fully cooked.

Nutritional value per serving: Calories: 146 kcal, Protein: 9g, Fat: 8g, Carbs: 12g

Country Style Ratatouille

It takes work to make a good ratatouille; but it is easy to do with some patience. The dish is so popular because it is so perfectly balanced in taste and textures.

Preparation time and cooking time: 1 hour and 20 minutes | Serves: 4

Ingredients To Use:

- 6 tablespoons olive oil, plus as needed
- 4 cloves garlic, chopped roughly
- 2 onion, sliced
- 2 large zucchini sliced into rounds 1/4-inch thick
- 2 medium eggplants, sliced into 1/2-inch thick rounds
- 2 cups chopped tomatoes
- 2 tablespoons Herbes de Provence
- 1/4 cup white wine (optional)
- Salt, to taste
- Pepper, to taste
- Chopped parsley, for garnish

Step-by-Step Directions to cook it:

1. Preheat your Lodge Cast Iron Dutch Oven.
2. Put 2 tablespoons olive oil into your pot.
3. Sauté zucchini until browned. Remove from pot.
4. Repeat process for eggplant, adding oil as needed to prevent burning. Remove from pot.
5. Repeat same process for onion until translucent. Remove from pot.
6. Put 2 tablespoons olive oil into the pot and sauté the garlic with tomatoes, herbs, salt and pepper (and wine if using). Stir and cook until softened.
7. Put cooked zucchini, eggplant and onions back into the pot. Stir well.
8. Cover and simmer gently or bake at 350°F for 20 minutes.

Nutritional value per serving: Calories: 247 kcal, Protein: 2.2g, Fat: 21.4g, Carbs: 12.7g

Kabocha Squash with Cumin

A good squash doesn't need a lot of extra bling to make its taste soar. With a dash of ground cumin, kombucha squash is a great side dish.

Preparation time and cooking time: 40 minutes | Serves: 4-6

Ingredients To Use:

- 2 tablespoons olive oil

- 2 to 3 kombucha squash

- 1 tablespoon ground cumin

- Sea salt

Step-by-Step Directions to cook it:

1.Preheat your Lodge Cast Iron Dutch Oven.
2.Cut squash in half, spoon out seeds.
3.Rub with olive oil, inside and out.
4.Sprinkle inside with ground cumin and salt.
5.Turn flat face down on bottom of pot.
6.Bake at 350°F for 30 minutes or until tender.

*Nutritional value per serving:*Calories: 134 kcal, Protein: 2.8g, Fat: 3.8g, Carbs: 26.1 g

Sassy Succotash

Succotash is a colorful dish that blends the textures and flavors of corn, bean and okra. From crunchy to creamy to tender, each mouthful will be a delight.

Preparation time and cooking time: 30 minutes | Serves: 4-6

Ingredients To Use:

- 2 tablespoons olive oil
- 2 cups lima beans, cooked
- 1 ham hock, smoked; OR 4 slices bacon, chopped
- 2 cups okra, chopped
- 2 cups corn kernels
- 1 onion, chopped
- 1 cup cherry tomatoes, sliced
- Salt and pepper, to taste
- 2 tablespoons salted butter

Step-by-Step Directions to cook it:

1. Preheat your Lodge Cast Iron Dutch Oven.
2. Heat oil for 30 seconds on medium heat, then add onions and stir.
3. Add bacon or ham hock, okra, corn and onions. Stir, sautéing for 10 minutes.
4. Add lima beans and tomatoes and stir, sautéing for 10 more minutes.
5. Before serving, add butter, salt and pepper.

Nutritional value per serving: Calories: 213 kcal, Protein: 26.5g, Fat: 12.9g, Carbs: 174g

Chapter 6: Soups, Stews, & Broths Recipes

Chili Con Carne

We call it Chili Con Carne. Whatever you know this as a universal language is the alluring scent as a pot of Chilli bubbles away on the burner!!

Preparation time and cooking time: 1 hour & 20 minutes | Serves: 6

Ingredients To Use:

- Spice packet
- 1 teaspoon salt
- ½ teaspoon freshly ground black pepper
- 2 ½ teaspoons ground cumin
- 1 ½ teaspoon chili powder
- 1 teaspoon crushed chilies
- 1 tablespoon paprika
- 1 tablespoon dried oregano
- 1 cinnamon stick
- 1 bay leaf
- 1 ½ pound lean ground beef
- 1 large onion, chopped
- 3 cloves garlic, chopped
- 2 (14.5-ounce) cans diced tomatoes with liquid
- 1 (15-ounce) can red kidney beans, rinsed and drained
- 1 (15-ounce) can black beans, rinsed and drained

Step-by-Step Directions to cook it:

1. At home, combine the necessary spices in a lidded container or resealable bag.
2. At the campsite, place your 12-inch Lodge Cast Iron Dutch Oven over 18 briquettes.
3. Sauté the ground beef until it is browned and drain any excess grease.
4. Add the onion and cook until it is tender, then stir in the garlic. Add the spices and tomatoes.
5. Cover the pot, and arrange it with 16 briquettes underneath and 8 on top. Cook for 45 minutes, maintaining a temperature around 325°F.
6. Add the beans and cook for 15 more minutes. Remove the cinnamon stick and bay leaf before serving.

Nutritional value per serving: Calories: 318 kcal, Protein: 19.4g, Fat: 12.4g, Carbs: 30.1g

Campfire Chicken and Dumplings

If you don't happen to have a campfire nearby, this recipe can easily be made indoors on the stove. Using homemade chicken stock for the finest performance.

Preparation time and cooking time: 55 minutes | Serves: 6

Ingredients To Use:

- 1 whole fryer chicken, 4-5 pounds
- 4 stalks celery, sliced
- 1 large onion, diced
- 2 medium carrots, peeled and sliced

- 1 teaspoon salt
- 1 teaspoon black pepper
- 2 teaspoons garlic powder
- 1 (14.5-ounce) can low-Sodium chicken broth

For the dumplings

- 1 ½ cups white whole wheat flour
- ½ teaspoon salt
- 5 tablespoons butter

- 1 egg
- ½ cup milk
- 1 tablespoon dried parsley

Step-by-Step Directions to cook it:

1. Preheat your Lodge Cast Iron Dutch Oven.
2. Using a pot, add the chicken with enough water to just cover. Put in the celery, onion, carrots, salt, black pepper, and broth.
3. Bring the pot to a boil and then transfer it to less intense heat. Keep it simmering for an hour.
4. Meanwhile, prepare the dumpling batter. Combine the flour and salt and cut in the butter. Mix in the egg, milk, parsley, and pepper, and knead for about 5 minutes.
5. Carefully remove the chicken to a strainer and let it cool a little. Remove and discard any skin and fat, and pull the meat from the bones.
6. Skim the fat from the broth and add the cooked chicken back in. Taste the broth and add more seasonings if desired.
7. Pull off little bits of the dumpling dough and roll them into balls if desired. Drop them into the broth.
8. Cover the pot and bring it to a simmer. Cook, covered, for 20 minutes.

Nutritional value per serving: Calories: 463 kcal, Protein: 50.1g, Fat: 16.3g, Carbs: 25.2g

Tomato Chickpea Soup

This is the greatest soup for the pantry. I am also betting that most of you already have these ingredients on hand. We're all about fresh food around here, but from time to time, there's nothing wrong with opening up a few cans.

Preparation time and cooking time: 40 minutes | Serves: 8

Ingredients To Use:

- ¼ cup extra-virgin olive oil
- 2 medium yellow onions, diced
- 1 stalk celery, diced
- 4 cloves garlic, minced
- 1 bunch kale, trimmed and chopped (about 3 cups)
- 2 (28-ounce) cans crushed tomatoes
- 1 quart low-Sodium vegetable stock
- 1 cup basmati rice, rinsed
- ¼ cup tomato paste
- 2 (15-ounce) cans chickpeas, drained and rinsed
- 1 teaspoon salt
- ½ teaspoon black pepper
- Hot sauce or crushed chilies, to taste

Step-by-Step Directions to cook it:

1. Preheat your Lodge Cast Iron Dutch Oven.
2. Using a pot, warm the oil and sauté the onion and celery for 3–5 minutes. Stir in the garlic and cook until fragrant.
3. Add the kale, and stir for a minute or two until it begins to wilt.
4. Add the tomatoes, vegetable stock, and rice. Bring the mixture to a boil and let it simmer for 15–20 minutes.
5. Add the tomato paste, chickpeas, salt, pepper, and hot sauce. Cook to heat through, and serve.

Nutritional value per serving: Calories: 323 kcal, Protein: 11.6g, Fat: 9.3g, Carbs: 52.9g

Spiced Lentil Soup

I've made some mediocre lentil soups over the years that have never seen the light of day on this website.

Preparation time and cooking time: 35 minutes | Serves: 4

Ingredients To Use:

- •Spice packet
- •2 teaspoons ground turmeric
- •1 ½ teaspoons ground cumin
- •¼ teaspoon cinnamon
- •½ teaspoon sea salt
- •½ teaspoon black pepper
- •Pinch red pepper flakes
- •2 tablespoons extra virgin olive oil

- •1 large onion, diced
- •3 cloves garlic, minced
- •¾ cup red lentils, rinsed and drained
- •1 (15-ounce) can diced tomatoes, with juices
- •1 (15-ounce) can light coconut milk
- •1 quart low-Sodium vegetable broth
- •3 cups packed baby spinach
- •1 tablespoon fresh lemon juice

Step-by-Step Directions to cook it:

1. Preheat your Lodge Cast Iron Dutch Oven.
2. Combine the spices in a small, lidded container, and seal.
3. Using a pot, warm the oil and sauté the onion and garlic until tender.
4. Add the spices and the lentils and mix well. Continue cooking for another minute or two, but don't let the spices burn.
5. Add the tomatoes, coconut milk, and broth. Bring it to a boil and simmer, uncovered, for 20 minutes, or until the lentils are tender.
6. Add the spinach and lemon juice, and cook until the spinach wilts.

Nutritional value per serving: Calories: 254 kcal, Protein: 7.3g, Fat: 14.9g, Carbs: 25.4g

Fireman's Spicy Stew

When firemen aren't busy battling flames, this spicy, vegetable-rich chicken stew fights their own rumbling stomachs.

Preparation time and cooking time: 1 hour & 50 minutes | Serves: 12

Ingredients To Use:

- 1 teaspoon oregano, dried
- 4 garlic cloves, minced
- 2 tablespoons ground cumin
- 2 tablespoons ground coriander
- 3 tablespoons chili powder
- 1 can (14 ½ ounces each) beef broth
- 3 cans (14 ½ ounces each) stewed tomatoes, diced
- 4 cans (16 ounces each) kidney beans, rinsed and drained
- 1 medium green pepper, chopped
- 2 medium onions, chopped
- 4 pounds (90%) lean ground beef
- 2 tablespoons olive oil

Step-by-Step Directions to cook it:

1. Preheat your Lodge Cast Iron Dutch Oven.
2. Using a pot, heat up olive oil over medium heat in your Lodge Cast Iron Dutch Oven
3. Add beef in batches and brown them, making sure to crumble the meat in the process until they are no longer pink
4. Drain any excess oil and keep the meat on the side
5. Add onions, green pepper, cook until fragrant and shows a nice soft texture
6. Re-introduce the meat to the oven and stir in remaining ingredients
7. Bring the mix to a boil and lower heat, simmer (covered) for about 1 and ½ hours until thoroughly cooked and the flavors have blended in
8. Enjoy!

Nutritional value per serving: Calories: 443 kcal, Protein: 27g, Fat: 27g, Carbs: 15g

Creamy Bacon And Potato Soup

An simple and tasty recipe for creamy potato soup that can be made in only one pot! Packed with bacon and fluffy potato goodness, in my household, this is a favorite comfort food.

Preparation time and cooking time: 55 minutes | Serves: 4

Ingredients To Use:

- ¼ teaspoon pepper
- 1 teaspoon salt
- 1 tablespoon fresh chives, chopped
- ¼ cup flour
- 1 cup cheddar cheese, shredded
- 2 cups of water

- 2 cups whole milk
- 1 onion, chopped
- 10 garlic cloves, minced
- 2 pounds large russet potatoes, peeled and cut up into 1/2 inch pieces
- 6 piece bacon slices
- 1 whole onion, chopped

Step-by-Step Directions to cook it:

1. Preheat your Lodge Cast Iron Dutch Oven.
2. Heat a pot over medium heat
3. Add bacon and cook for about 10-15 minutes until crispy
4. Transfer to a paper towel and drain excess grease
5. Once cooled, crumbled into small pieces
6. Add onions to your pot alongside bacon grease
7. Cook for about 5 minutes until tender, making sure to stir from time to time
8. Add flour and remaining ingredients, stir cook for 3 minutes
9. Add water and stir until everything is mixed well
10. Add milk and stir, bring the mix to a boil over high heat
11. Lower down the heat to medium-low and let the mixture simmer for about 15 minutes
12. Make sure to keep stirring it in order to prevent the potatoes from burning
13. Once done, serve in bowls with a topping of bacon crumbles, chopped chives, and cheddar
14. Enjoy!

Nutritional value per serving: Calories: 1549 kcal, Protein: 27g, Fat: 25g, Carbs: 53g

Bacon And Carrot Cheese Soup

Thick and delicious, bacon and carrot soup is a comfort food that warms the soul! Connect with a nice dose of sharp cheddar cheese and just a little bacon, and you'll have a nice winter dinner on the table.

Preparation time and cooking time: 3 hours and 15 minutes | Serves: 4

Ingredients To Use:

- Salt and pepper to taste
- 1-pound small baby potatoes
- 2 bunch of small carrots, tops cut
- 2 cups beef broth
- 5 sprigs thyme

- 1/3 cup balsamic vinegar
- 2-3 tablespoon Dijon mustard
- 1 medium yellow onion, chopped
- 4 pounds Chuck roast
- 2-3 tablespoon vegetable/ olive oil

Step-by-Step Directions to cook it:

1. Pre-heat your oven to a temperature of 300 degrees F
2. Heat up a pot over high heat and add oil, let the oil heat up
3. Season chuck roast generously with salt and pepper
4. Add to the pan and brown all sides (2-3 minutes per side)
5. Add chopped onions to the drippings and lower down the heat to medium
6. Add onions and Saute them for 5 minutes until tender
7. Add vinegar and increase the heat to medium-high
8. Bring to a boil and keep boiling until the mixture is slightly syrupy like
9. Add Dijon and stir
10. Add 2 cups beef broth and thyme sprigs
11. Place lid and transfer to oven, bake for 2 ½ - 3 hours until it shows a nice tender texture
12. Add carrots, potatoes to your pot and return to the oven once again
13. Cook for 30-60 minutes more until they are nice and tender
14. Season according to your taste and serve
15. Enjoy!

Nutritional value per serving: Calories: 510 kcal, Protein: 14g, Fat: 20g, Carbs: 40g

Creamy Broccoli Soup

This lightened-up broccoli soup uses the starch in a potato and a quick round of blending to achieve a smooth mouthfeel. Adding the broccoli in the beginning dulls the color, so I like to wait until the end of cooking to preserve some of the vegetable's vibrancy.

Preparation time and cooking time: 35 minutes | Serves: 6

Ingredients To Use:

- ¼ cup olive oil
- ½ white onion, chopped
- 2 celery stalks, chopped
- 2 carrots, chopped
- 2½ teaspoons salt
- 1 small russet potato, chopped

- 2 garlic cloves, minced
- 4 cups vegetable stock
- 1 large head broccoli, chopped (5 cups florets)
- ½ cup shredded cheddar cheese (optional)

Step-by-Step Directions to cook it:

1. Preheat your Lodge Cast Iron Dutch Oven.
2. Heat a pot over medium heat. Add the olive oil, onion, celery, carrots, and salt. Sauté for 3 minutes, stirring occasionally to prevent browning.
3. Cook the potato. Add the potato and garlic. Sauté for about 7 minutes or until the potato softens and cooks through, stirring occasionally.
4. Simmer and blend with the broccoli. Add the vegetable stock, increase the heat to medium-high, and bring the soup to a simmer. Cook for 8 minutes. Turn off the heat and use a slotted spoon to transfer the cooked vegetables to a blender. Scoop out about 2 cups of liquid from the pot and add it to the blender. Add the broccoli florets to the blender and blend on high speed until the mixture is very smooth and creamy.
5. Return the creamy soup to the pot and serve. Pour the blended soup back into the Lodge Cast Iron Dutch Oven and bring it to a simmer. Stir well, then turn off the heat to preserve the broccoli's color. You can add cheddar cheese (if using) to the soup in the Lodge Cast Iron Dutch Oven, or you can serve the soup and garnish with the cheese. Refrigerate leftovers for easy reheating for up to 3 days.

Nutritional value per serving: Calories: 270 kcal, Protein: 12g, Fat: 18g, Carbs: 17g

Vegetable and Lentil Soup

This simple dish draws a lot of bold flavor from garam masala, a blend of toasted spices. Spices cooked down with vegetables and lentils are all you need to turn simple ingredients into a meal.

Preparation time and cooking time: 35 minutes | Serves: 6

Ingredients To Use:

- 3 tablespoons olive oil
- 1 onion, chopped
- 2 carrots, chopped
- 2 celery stalks, chopped
- 1 tablespoon garam masala, plus more for seasoning
- 1 tablespoon salt, plus more for seasoning
- 2 teaspoons curry powder, plus more for seasoning
- 1 teaspoon freshly ground black pepper, plus more for seasoning
- 6 cups filtered water
- 2 cups red or yellow lentils

Step-by-Step Directions to cook it:

1. Preheat your Lodge Cast Iron Dutch Oven.
2. In a pot over medium heat, warm the olive oil. Add the onion, carrots, and celery. Sweat the vegetables for 7 minutes, stirring occasionally. Stir in the garam masala, salt, curry powder, and pepper. Cook for about 2 minutes, until aromatic.
3. Simmer the lentils. Pour the water over the vegetables and add the lentils. Stir, then cover the pot and simmer, stirring occasionally, for about 15 minutes, until the lentils are tender and cooked through.
4. Adjust the seasoning and serve. Taste the soup and add more salt or spices as desired. Ladle the soup into bowls and top as desired. Refrigerate leftovers for up to 3 days

Nutritional value per serving: Calories: 193 kcal, Protein: 12g, Fat: 5g, Carbs: 26g

Pork Green Chili

This fun green chili is loaded with complex flavors from the slow-cooked pork shoulder, aromatic spices, and tangy, spicy green chiles. It's an easy restaurant-quality dish I love to show off when cooking for family or friends.

Preparation time and cooking time: 1 hour and 50 minutes | Serves: 6

Ingredients To Use:

- 2 tablespoons olive oil
- 2 pounds boneless pork shoulder
- 2 teaspoons salt
- 1 teaspoon dried oregano
- 1 teaspoon ground cumin
- 1 teaspoon onion powder
- 1 teaspoon ground coriander
- 1 cup salsa verde
- ½ cup sour cream
- 1 (4-ounce) can diced green chiles
- 1 cup filtered water
- 1 (15-ounce) can black beans, drained and rinsed

Step-by-Step Directions to cook it:

1. Preheat your Lodge Cast Iron Dutch Oven.
2. Cook the pork. Cut the pork shoulder into cubes, roughly 1 inch thick. In a pot over medium heat, warm the olive oil. Add the pork and season with the salt. Sear for 3 minutes to brown the meat on all sides, turning it with a spatula.
3. Add the spices and other ingredients, then simmer. Stir in the oregano, cumin, onion powder, and coriander. Cook for 30 seconds, until aromatic. Pour in the salsa verde, sour cream, green chiles, and water. Stir to combine, scraping along the bottom of the pot with a wooden spoon or spatula to release any browned bits. Cover the pot and reduce the heat to medium-low. Simmer the soup for 1½ hours or until the pork is tender and shreds easily with a fork.
4. Add the black beans, adjust seasonings, and serve. Add the black beans and bring the soup back to a simmer. Taste and adjust the seasoning as desired. Ladle into bowls and garnish with cilantro (if using) and cheese (if using). Refrigerate leftovers for up to 4 days.

Nutritional value per serving: Calories: 538 kcal, Protein: 38g, Fat: 28g, Carbs: 34g

Turmeric Vegetable Soup

I like to call this my immunity-boosting soup because the spices stimulate the immune system and turmeric is known for its anti-inflammatory properties.

Preparation time and cooking time: 30 minutes | Serves: 6

Ingredients To Use:

• 2 tablespoons olive oil

• 1 sweet potato, peeled and diced

• 1 teaspoon salt, plus more for seasoning

• 5 garlic cloves, minced

• 1 poblano chile, seeded and chopped

• 2 cups frozen corn

• 1 tablespoon chili powder

• 1 teaspoon ground cumin

• 1 teaspoon ground turmeric

• ½ cup dry white wine

• 4 cups water

• 1 (14-ounce) can coconut milk

Step-by-Step Directions to cook it:

1. Preheat your Lodge Cast Iron Dutch Oven.
2. Sauté the vegetables. In a pot over medium heat, warm the olive oil. Add the sweet potato and salt. Stir to combine and cook for 7 minutes or until the potato begins to brown. Stir in the garlic, poblano, and corn. Cook for 3 minutes more.
3. Deglaze and simmer. Add the chili powder, cumin, and turmeric, and toss to coat the vegetables. Cook for 1 minute. Stir in the white wine and deglaze the pot, scraping along the bottom of the pot to release any browned bits. Add the water and increase the heat to medium-high. Bring the soup to a simmer and cook for about 5 minutes, until heated through.
4. Season and serve. Turn off the heat and stir in the coconut milk. Taste and, if the soup is bland, season with salt. Refrigerate leftovers for up to 3 days.

Nutritional value per serving: Calories: 950 kcal, Protein: 51g, Fat: 18g, Carbs: 160g

Chapter 7: Beans & Eggs

Sautéed Chard with Cannellini Beans

Combining greens, especially chard, with beans is common in Italian cuisine. The combination is served alone, or with pasta for a more substantial dish. Most recipes call for discarding the stems of the chard, which I think is a mistake.

Preparation time and cooking time: 60 minutes | Serves: 2

Ingredients To Use:

- 1 bunch red or rainbow chard
- 2 to 3 tablespoons olive oil
- ½ small onion, chopped
- 2 garlic cloves, chopped
- Kosher salt
- ¼ cup dry white wine

- 1 medium tomato, seeded and diced
- 2 tablespoons diced or puréed sun-dried tomatoes
- ¼ teaspoon red pepper flakes
- 1 (14-ounce) can cannellini beans, drained and rinsed

Step-by-Step Directions to cook it:

1. Preheat your Lodge Cast Iron Dutch Oven.
2. Rinse the chard and cut the leaves from the stems. Dice enough of the stems to make ½ cup; reserve the rest for another use or discard. Stack the leaves up and cut into ½-inch ribbons.
3. Add olive oil in the pot over medium heat. Heat until the oil shimmers and then add the onion, garlic, and chard stems. Season with salt and cook, stirring, for 5 to 6 minutes, or until the onion pieces have separated and the chard has softened.
4. Add the wine and bring to a simmer. Add the diced tomato, sun-dried tomatoes, and red pepper flakes.
5. Add the chard leaves by big handfuls, stirring to wilt. When all the chard is added, bring to a simmer and cover the pot. Cook for about 15 minutes, or until the chard is very soft. Taste and adjust the seasoning, adding more salt or red pepper flakes if necessary. Add the beans and cook for another 5 minutes, or until the beans are heated through.

Nutritional value per serving: Calories: 220.4 kcal, Protein: 9.6g, Fat: 4.3g, Carbs: 38.3g

Mexican Red Rice and Beans

In my search for delicious Mexican red rice, also known as Spanish rice, I tried a couple of recipes, one from author and restaurateur Rick Bayless, and another from writer Sandra Gutierrez, who specializes in Latin American cuisine.

Preparation time and cooking time: 75 minutes | Serves: 2

Ingredients To Use:

- 2 to 3 tablespoons olive oil
- ½ small onion, chopped (about ⅓ cup)
- 1 large garlic clove, minced
- 1 small jalapeño pepper, seeded and chopped (about 1 tablespoon)
- ½ cup long-grain white rice
- 3 tablespoons red salsa
- 2 tablespoons tomato sauce
- ¾ cup vegetable stock
- ¼ teaspoon ground cumin
- ½ teaspoon kosher salt
- 1 (14-ounce) can pinto beans, drained and rinsed
- 1 tablespoon chopped fresh parsley

Step-by-Step Directions to cook it:

1. Preheat the Lodge Cast Iron Dutch Oven to 350°F.
2. Place the pot over medium heat. Add enough oil to coat the bottom of the pot and heat until the oil shimmers. Add the onion, garlic, and jalapeño and cook, stirring, for 4 to 5 minutes, or until the onion pieces have separated and the vegetables have softened. Add the rice and stir to coat. Cook for about 1 minute.
3. Add the salsa, tomato sauce, vegetable stock, cumin, salt, and beans and stir to combine. Bring the liquid to a strong simmer and cover.
4. Place the pot in the oven and cook for 18 minutes. Remove from the oven and let sit, covered, for 15 minutes. Remove the lid and add the parsley. Gently toss the rice with two large forks to fluff the rice and mix in the parsley.

Nutritional value per serving: Calories: 210.3 kcal, Protein: 4g, Fat: 7.9g, Carbs: 29.5g

Baked Eggs Florentine

Bacon and spinach go together deliciously, and the addition of heavy cream, eggs, and cheese make this a downright decadent dish.

Preparation time and cooking time: 40 minutes | Serves: 2

Ingredients To Use:

- 2 to 3 slices bacon, diced
- 1 pound baby spinach
- ¾ cup heavy cream
- 2 garlic cloves, minced
- Kosher salt

- ⅛ teaspoon freshly ground white or black pepper
- 2 teaspoons butter, melted
- 3 tablespoons grated Parmigiano-Reggiano or similar cheese
- ½ cup panko bread crumbs
- 2 to 4 large eggs

Step-by-Step Directions to cook it:

1. Preheat the oven to 375°F.
2. Place the pot over medium heat. Add the bacon and stir to separate the pieces. Cook, stirring occasionally, until the bacon is crisp and has rendered most of its fat. Remove the bacon pieces to a paper towel–lined plate, leaving the fat in the pot.
3. By the handful, add the spinach to the pot, stirring to wilt it, and adding more as soon as there is room. It should take 4 batches or so. Remove the spinach to a colander and press with the back of a large spoon to drain off as much liquid as possible.
4. Pour the cream into the pot and add the garlic. Cook for 3 minutes, or until the cream has reduced by about one-third. Season with salt, stir in the pepper, and add the spinach back to the pot. Stir to distribute the cream and bring the mixture to a simmer.
5. While the mixture heats, in a small bowl, stir together the butter, cheese, and panko.

6. Sprinkle the reserved bacon over the surface of the spinach. With the back of the spoon, make an indentation in the spinach mixture for each egg you're using. (Depending on the size of your pot, the spinach might not be deep enough for this.) Crack the eggs into the indentations and sprinkle the panko mixture over the surface of the eggs, or the entire spinach mixture (if you have enough). Place the pot, uncovered, into the preheated oven. Bake for 8 to 10 minutes, or until the eggs are done to your liking.

7. To serve, spoon some spinach and eggs into two bowls, being careful not to break the eggs.

Nutritional value per serving: Calories: 266.9 kcal, Protein: 25.9g, Fat: 16.5g, Carbs: 3.4g

Shakshuka

Once in a while, a dish will become wildly popular, seemingly overnight. Shakshuka (also spelled shakshouka) is one of those dishes. Similar to "eggs in purgatory," this Middle Eastern spicy sauce and egg dish sometimes contains feta cheese.

Preparation time and cooking time: 40 minutes | Serves: 2

Ingredients To Use:

- 2 to 3 tbsp olive oil
- ½ small onion, chopped (about ⅓ cup)
- ½ medium red or green bell pepper, seeded and chopped (about ⅓ cup)
- 1 small jalapeño pepper
- 2 garlic cloves, chopped, divided
- Kosher salt
- 1 (14.5-ounce) can diced tomatoes with their juice
- ½ tsp. ground cumin
- ½ tsp. ground sweet paprika
- ¼ tsp. freshly ground black pepper
- ⅓ cup crumbled feta cheese
- 2 to 4 large eggs

Step-by-Step Directions to cook it:

1. Preheat your Lodge Cast Iron Dutch Oven
2. Set your pot over medium heat. Add enough oil to coat the bottom of the pot and heat until the oil shimmers. Add the onion, bell pepper, jalapeño, and half the garlic. Season with salt and cook, stirring occasionally, for about 10 minutes, or until the vegetables are soft.
3. Add the tomatoes, cumin, paprika, and black pepper and bring to a simmer. Cook for 10 minutes, stirring occasionally. Add the remaining garlic and cook for another 5 minutes. For a smoother consistency, use the back of a spoon or a potato masher to break up the tomatoes. Taste and adjust the seasoning. Gently stir in the feta cheese.
4. With the sauce still at a simmer, gently crack the eggs onto the surface. Cover and cook for about 3 minutes, then remove the cover. Baste the tops of the eggs with some of the sauce and cook until the eggs are done to your liking, 3 to 5 more minutes, continuing to baste once or twice more.

Nutritional value per serving: Calories: 298 kcal, Protein: 17g, Fat: 19g, Carbs: 16g

Corned Beef Hash with Eggs

Preparation time and cooking time: 40 minutes | Serves: 2

Ingredients To Use:

- 2 to 3 tablespoons olive or vegetable oil
- 1 to 2 small Yukon Gold potatoes diced into ¼-inch cubes
- 1 very small onion, diced (about ½ cup)
- Kosher salt
- 6 ounces (about 2 cups) cooked corned beef, diced into ¼-inch cubes
- ½ cup chicken or beef stock
- 1 to 2 tablespoons heavy cream
- Freshly ground black pepper
- 2 to 4 large eggs

Step-by-Step Directions to cook it:

1. Preheat the oven to 375°F.
2. Set a pot over medium heat. Add enough oil to coat the bottom of the pot and heat until the oil shimmers. Add the potatoes in a single layer and cook without stirring for 3 to 4 minutes, or until the bottoms are browned. Use a spatula to flip over the potatoes, then brown for a minute or two and flip again. Try to brown all sides of the potato cubes until they're crispy.
3. If there is still some oil in the pot, add the onion. If the skillet is dry, move the potatoes to the sides of the pan, add another tablespoon of oil in the center, and heat for a minute before adding the onion. Season with salt. Cook, stirring gently, until the onion pieces separate and soften. Try not to break the potato pieces apart.
4. Add the corned beef and stock and bring the liquid to a simmer, reducing slightly. Stir in the cream and season with salt and black pepper. The hash ingredients should be coated generously with sauce, but not swimming in liquid.
5. If possible, make 2 or 4 indentations in the hash for the eggs. (Depending on the size of your pot, the hash ingredients might not be deep enough for this.) Crack the eggs into the indentations and place the pot, uncovered, into the preheated oven. Bake for 8 to 10 minutes, or until the eggs are done to your liking.
6. Let cool slightly and serve.

Nutritional value per serving: Calories: 631 kcal, Protein: 28g, Fat: 51g, Carbs: 16g

Root Vegetable Hash and Scrambled Eggs

Perfectly meatless, this nutritious, colorful, and hearty hash-and-egg combo makes breakfast (or breakfast for dinner) worth waiting for. Unlike the Corned Beef Hash with Eggs, this dish is cooked mostly in the oven, which means it requires very little hands-on work.

Preparation time and cooking time: 1 hour and 20 minutes | Serves: 4

Ingredients To Use:

- 1 very small red beet
- 1 very small sweet potato
- 1 small Yukon Gold potato
- 1 medium carrot
- ½ medium onion, coarsely chopped
- 2 to 3 tablespoons olive oil
- ¼ teaspoon kosher salt, plus more for sprinkling
- 1 tablespoon butter
- 3 to 4 large eggs
- Freshly ground black pepper
- ¼ cup grated Parmigiano-Reggiano or similar cheese

Step-by-Step Directions to cook it:

1. Preheat the oven to 375°F.
2. Peel the beet, sweet potato, gold potato, and carrot and cut them into pieces about ½ inch on a side.
3. Add the cut vegetables along with the onion to the pot and drizzle with enough olive oil to coat all the vegetables. Sprinkle with salt and toss to coat. Move the vegetables into an even layer.
4. Place the pot, uncovered, in the hot oven and roast for about 20 minutes. Remove the pot and stir the vegetables. Return to the oven and roast for another 15 minutes and stir again. Check one of the beet chunks with a small knife or fork to see if it's tender; if not, continue to cook for 10 to 15 minutes. The vegetables should be crisp on the outside but soft inside.

5. Place the pot over medium-low heat and move the hash to the perimeter of the pot. Add the butter to the center of the pot.
6. In a small bowl, whisk together the eggs with the remaining ¼ teaspoon of salt while the butter melts. When it's foaming, pour the eggs in and let sit for 30 seconds or so, just until they start to set. Stir the eggs for 1 to 2 minutes. Sprinkle the eggs and vegetables with the pepper and cheese, and either mix the eggs into the vegetables or serve separately.

Nutritional value per serving: Calories: 279 kcal, Protein: 9g, Fat: 18g, Carbs: 23g

Leek and Red Pepper Frittata

Frittatas, the Italian cousins to French omelets, are ordinarily made in a skillet using the Lodge Cast Iron Dutch Oven, although they are often finished in the oven. A Lodge Cast Iron Dutch Oven works well for cooking a frittata, with a couple of adjustments.

Preparation time and cooking time: 45 minutes | Serves: 2

Ingredients To Use:

•3 tbsp. butter

•1 small leek, washed, trimmed, and chopped (white and light green parts only)

•½ small red bell pepper, seeded and chopped

•Kosher salt

•5 large eggs

•2 tbsp. whole milk

•Freshly ground black pepper

•½ cup shredded Fontina cheese (or other mild, melting cheese)

Step-by-Step Directions to cook it:

1.Preheat the oven to 325°F.
2.Place the pot over medium heat and add the butter. When it stops foaming, add the leek and bell pepper and season with salt. Cook, stirring, for 3 to 4 minutes, or until the vegetables have softened. Spread them evenly over the bottom of the pot. Turn the heat to low.
3.In a bowl, whisk together the eggs and milk, and season with salt and pepper. Pour into the pot. Cook over low heat for 2 to 3 minutes, or until the bottom of the eggs set slightly.
4.Move the pot into the oven and cook, uncovered, for 10 to 15 minutes, or until the eggs are beginning to set, with the middle not yet done. Remove from the oven, sprinkle the cheese over the frittata and return to bake for another 5 minutes, or until the cheese is melted and the eggs are just barely set.
5.Remove from the oven and use a silicone spatula to divide the frittata into 4 to 6 pieces. Remove the slices from the pot. Let cool slightly. Serve warm or at room temperature.

Nutritional value per serving: Calories: 292 kcal, Protein: 12.1g, Fat: 14.6g, Carbs: 29g

Congee with Eggs and Herbs

Congee, or rice porridge, comes in several different varieties, both sweet and savory. Sometimes it's cooked until it's smooth and silky; other times it's thicker and more rustic.

Preparation time and cooking time: 1 hour | Serves: 2

Ingredients To Use:

- ¼ cup Arborio rice (or long grain)
- 3 cups water
- ½ tsp. kosher salt
- 2 eggs
- 1 tbsp. coarsely chopped fresh cilantro
- 1 tbsp. minced fresh chives
- 1 to 2 tsp. hot chili oil or sesame oil (optional)

Step-by-Step Directions to cook it:

1. Preheat your Lodge Cast Iron Dutch Oven.
2. Place the rice in a strainer and rinse well. Add the rice, water, and salt to a pot and cover. Place over medium-high heat and wait for it to boil. As soon as the water boils, reduce the heat to low and stir the mixture. Cover and simmer for about 45 minutes, stirring every 15 minutes or so to keep the rice from sticking. After 45 minutes, the rice should be very soft and the porridge should have a silky consistency. If not, cook for another 10 minutes or so.
3. While the porridge cooks, whisk together the two eggs in a small bowl.
4. When the rice is cooked, slowly pour the egg into the porridge in a thin stream. If you want a custardy texture, whisk the mixture quickly while you pour in the egg. If you prefer ribbons of egg, stir more slowly. Cook for a minute or two or until the egg is done.
5. Stir in the cilantro and chives, and drizzle over the oil (if using).

Nutritional value per serving: Calories: 150 kcal, Protein: 3g, Fat: 3.5g, Carbs: 27g

Baked Oatmeal with Blueberries and Apples

This version of oatmeal is more like a soft breakfast bar with fruit than porridge. It makes a good addition to a brunch or breakfast buffet.

Preparation time and cooking time: 1 hour | Serves: 2

Ingredients To Use:

- 1 to 2 tablespoons butter
- ½ Gala apple, peeled, cored and cut into ½-inch pieces
- ½ cup fresh blueberries
- 1 tablespoon maple syrup
- ⅔ cup uncooked rolled oats
- ¼ cup blanched slivered almonds
- ¼ teaspoon baking powder
- ¼ teaspoon cinnamon
- Pinch kosher salt
- ⅔ cup whole milk
- 1 egg yolk
- 2 teaspoons brown sugar
- ¼ teaspoon vanilla extract

Step-by-Step Directions to cook it:

1. Heat up the oven to 375°F.
2. Butter the bottom of a pot about 1 inch up the sides. Add the apple and blueberries in a thin layer. Drizzle with the maple syrup.
3. In a bowl, mix together the oats, almonds, baking powder, cinnamon, and salt.
4. In a small bowl, whisk together the milk, egg yolk, sugar, and vanilla and pour over the oat mixture. Stir just until combined and spoon over the fruit.
5. Bake, uncovered, for 30 to 35 minutes, or until the top is golden brown and the fruit is bubbling. Let cool for 10 to 15 minutes before serving.

Nutritional value per serving: Calories: 390 kcal, Protein: 12.9g, Fat: 22.5g, Carbs: 35.1 g

Chapter 8: Desserts & Snacks

Crispy Salt & Vinegar Chickpeas

Roasted chickpeas are one of my favorite snacks. You can make them in the oven, but they come out even better when you make them in an air fryer. They're crispy outside, creamy inside, and you can change the seasonings to match your mood.

Preparation time and cooking time: 20 minutes | Serves: 6

Ingredients To Use:

•1 (15-ounce) can low-sodium chickpeas, drained

•1 tablespoon malt vinegar or distilled white vinegar

•½ teaspoon extra-virgin olive oil

•½ teaspoon Celtic sea salt

Step-by-Step Directions to cook it:

1.In a small bowl, stir together the chickpeas, vinegar, olive oil, and salt. Mix well. Transfer the chickpeas to your oven. Fry at 370°F for 15 minutes, shaking the basket halfway through the cooking time.
2.Let the chickpeas cool in a single layer. They will continue to crisp as they cool.
3.To store, drain, as needed. Refrigerate, covered, for 3 to 5 days, or freeze for up to 3 months.

Nutritional value per serving: Calories: 99 kcal, Protein: 4g, Fat: 1g, Carbs: 14g

Baba Ghanoush

Baba ghanoush is a dip that's similar to hummus, but made with roasted eggplant instead of chickpeas. Whoever invented it is a genius—eggplant gives the dip a silky texture and mildly floral flavor.

Preparation time and cooking time: 20 minutes | Serves: 6

Ingredients To Use:

• 1 large (about 1 pound) globe eggplant, cut into ½-inch-thick rounds

• 2 tablespoons tahini

• 2 garlic cloves, peeled

• Juice of 1 lemon

• ¼ cup fresh cilantro or parsley

• 1 teaspoon Celtic sea salt

• Pinch ground cumin

• 1 teaspoon extra-virgin olive oil

Step-by-Step Directions to cook it:

1. Preheat the Lodge Cast Iron Dutch Oven.
2. Place the eggplant rounds on a sheet pan. Broil for 10 minutes until soft and golden brown. Scoop the eggplant into a blender, discarding the skin.
3. Add the tahini, garlic, lemon juice, cilantro, salt, and cumin. Blend into a thick paste. Scrape the dip into a bowl and drizzle with the olive oil. Cover and refrigerate until ready to serve. The baba ghanoush will keep, refrigerated, for 3 to 5 days.

Nutritional value per serving: Calories: 64 kcal, Protein: 2g, Fat: 4g, Carbs: 3g

Small-Batch Buttermilk Biscuits

These biscuits complement many of the recipes in this book (try them with the Mexi-Egg Scramble, or Smoky Split Pea Soup with Bacon). They contain only four ingredients and are perfect with soups and stews as well as slathered with butter.

Preparation time and cooking time: 15 minutes | Serves: 4

Ingredients To Use:

• 1¼ cups self-rising flour (store-bought or homemade), plus a little extra

• ¼ teaspoon salt

• 4 tablespoons butter

• ½ cup buttermilk, plus a few extra tablespoons for brushing the biscuits

Step-by-Step Directions to cook it:

1. Preheat the oven to 450°F. Line the bottom of a Lodge Cast Iron Dutch Oven with parchment paper.
2. In a medium bowl, whisk together the flour and salt. Cut in the butter using a pastry blender or two forks. Stir in the buttermilk. Mix gently until combined, making sure not to overmix.
3. Dust your hands with flour, then shape the dough into 6 mounds (about ⅓ cup each). Place them in the Lodge Cast Iron Dutch Oven. The dough mounds should be lightly touching each other. Brush each biscuit with buttermilk.
4. Bake for 10 to 15 minutes, uncovered, until the edges of the biscuits start to turn golden brown. Remove from the oven and serve warm or at room temperature.

Nutritional value per serving: Calories: 82 kcal, Protein: 1g, Fat: 2g, Carbs: 11g

Light and Soft Cranberry Scones

Scones are a great addition to a weekend brunch. I love having a scone in the morning with a cup of coffee or in the afternoon with a cup of tea.

Preparation time and cooking time: 5 minutes | Serves: 4

Ingredients To Use:

- •2 cups self-rising flour (store-bought or homemade)
- •½ cup sugar, plus a few extra tablespoons for sprinkling
- •½ cup salted butter, cold
- •¾ cup heavy (whipping) cream
- •⅔ cup sweetened dried cranberries
- •All-purpose flour, for dusting

Step-by-Step Directions to cook it:

1. Preheat the oven to 400°F.
2. In medium bowl, mix together the flour and sugar. Cut the cold butter into small pieces and add it to the flour. Mix with a pastry blender or two forks until the mixture resembles coarse crumbs. Add the cream, and mix it in with a spatula or wooden spoon until the dough is stiff. Knead in the cranberries.
3. On a piece of parchment paper dusted lightly with flour, shape the dough with your hands into an 8-inch disk. Gently slice the disk into 8 triangles, and slightly pull each away from the others so they are not touching. Lift the parchment paper, and gently place the whole thing, paper and all, into the Lodge Cast Iron Dutch Oven. Sprinkle with a little extra sugar.
4. Bake, uncovered, for about 20 minutes, until the scones are set in the center and slightly golden on top.
5. Remove the scones from the oven and let them cool in the pot for 10 minutes. Then, lift them out using the parchment paper, and transfer the whole package to a wire rack. Let cool for 10 more minutes before serving.

Nutritional value per serving: Calories: 87 kcal, Protein: 2.1g, Fat: 4.4g, Carbs: 10.3g

Strawberry Bread Pudding

Strawberries remind me of summer, but they are available all year round. Try and get the biggest, juiciest strawberries you can, because they will make this bread pudding delicious. If your market does not have fresh strawberries, you can use frozen ones, but make sure they are defrosted and drained before using them.

Preparation time and cooking time: 60 minutes | Serves: 4

Ingredients To Use:

- Nonstick cooking spray
- 3 cups whole milk
- ¾ cup sugar
- 4 eggs, beaten
- 1 (1-pound) loaf brioche or challah bread, cubed and dried out (see Tip)
- 2 cups sliced strawberries, plus more for serving

Step-by-Step Directions to cook it:

1. Preheat the Lodge Cast Iron Dutch Oven to 350°F. Spray a cooking pan generously with nonstick cooking spray.
2. In a large bowl, whisk together the milk, sugar, and eggs until well blended.
3. Place the bread cubes in the cooking pan, and spread them out evenly. Mix in the strawberries. Pour the milk mixture over the bread and strawberries. Let the mixture sit for 10 minutes so the bread can absorb the liquid.
4. Bake, uncovered, for about 45 minutes, until a fork or toothpick inserted into the middle comes out clean and the top is golden brown.
5. Cool for at least 10 minutes before serving.

Nutritional value per serving: Calories: 179.8 kcal, Protein: 7.1g, Fat: 4g, Carbs: 31.3g

Creamy Cinnamon Rice Pudding with Raisins

I grew up eating rice pudding; my mother made it often. To me it's a simple, old-fashioned comfort food. While my family likes to eat it cold, I especially love it warm.

Preparation time and cooking time: 40 minutes | Serves: 4

Ingredients To Use:

•6 cups whole milk

•1 cup medium-grain rice

•½ cup sugar

•1 teaspoon ground cinnamon, plus more for serving

•½ teaspoon salt

•½ cup raisins

Step-by-Step Directions to cook it:

1.Preheat your Lodge Cast Iron Dutch Oven.
2.Set a pot over medium-high heat, combine the milk, rice, sugar, cinnamon, salt, and raisins. Bring to a boil, stirring occasionally.
3.Reduce the heat to low and cook, uncovered, for 15 to 20 minutes, stirring often and scraping the sides and bottom of the pot with a wooden spoon, until the pudding is thick and creamy. (It will thicken more as it cools.) If it gets too thick, add a little extra milk.
4.Cool for 10 minutes before serving, or refrigerate until ready to serve. Sprinkle with extra cinnamon just before serving.

Nutritional value per serving: Calories: 309kcal, Protein: 8g, Fat: 10g, Carbs: 48g

Conclusion

Thank you for buying and reading Lodge Cast Iron Dutch Oven Cookbook, the source of a plethora of easy-to-make recipes fit for your budget and any cooking level. Throughout the book, you have had the opportunity to learn how to prepare some truly delicious meals right in the Lodge Cast Iron Dutch Oven.

Whether you want to treat yourself with a delicious breakfast, hearty main meal, tasty side dishes, or super yummy desserts, you have probably found what you were looking for in this book. Your Lodge Cast Iron Dutch Oven can help revolutionize the way you cook and prepare your meals. The beauty of the oven is that it can be used in a variety of settings ranging from your kitchen to a campsite.

Now all you have to do is to choose the recipe to turn into a delicious meal first. Lodge Cast Iron Dutch Oven allows users to experiment with different ingredients and explore a wide range of flavors. Use the recipes from this cookbook as an inspiration to focus on home-cooked meals and creating your own recipes that family and friends will enjoy.

Feel free to review and rate Lodge Cast Iron Dutch Oven Cookbook to help other people get motivated to start cooking just like you.

CPSIA information can be obtained
at www.ICGtesting.com
Printed in the USA
LVHW102326141021
700520LV00005B/65

9 781954 294516